THE A-Z OF GREAT CLASSROOMS

ROY BLATCHFORD

JOHN CATT

First Published 2023

by John Catt Educational Ltd,
15 Riduna Park, Station Road,
Melton, Woodbridge IP12 1QT

Tel: +44 (0) 1394 389850
Email: enquiries@johncatt.com
Website: www.johncatt.com

ISBN: 978 1 398388 40 6

Set and designed by John Catt Educational Limited

CONTENTS

FOREWORD

Many have attempted to distil the distinctive essence of the memorable classroom, but few capture its full colour, character, and complexity so adroitly.

If children are infected by the enthusiasm of their very best teachers, I defy any teacher to fail to be encouraged by the clarity, empathy, and enthusiasm across these pages.

From the first chapter, the author takes us beyond the familiar territory of simply setting out a series of practical tips and tactics. We are reminded of just how much underpins the rich repertoire of a great teacher – knowledge, presence, passion, values, creativity, empathy, resilience, reflection and – importantly – fun reverberate throughout these vignettes.

Roy Blatchford reminds us of the unseen magic that happens in our classrooms and corridors every day, and the importance of giving teachers the creative space to balance a professional vocation with their own personality and personal interests. We should all be encouraged and empowered to articulate a new narrative for our profession and, in doing so, shape our professional space.

In part guide and in part disguised memoir, these pages offer a combination of actionable insights and thoughtful reflections – what a gift to be able to distil a lifetime of experience such that it is equally powerful and provocative for both the novice and the experienced teacher. We would all be wise to heed the wisdom accrued across 15,000 lessons and 1,000 school settings.

This A–Z asks us all the question – do you see what I see, and if not, are you really looking?

Rebecca Boomer-Clark CEO, Academies Enterprise Trust

INTRODUCTION

Thomas More: Why not be a teacher? You'd be a fine teacher, perhaps a great one.

Richard Rich: If I was, who would know it?

Thomas More: You, your pupils, your friends, God. Not a bad public, that.

A Man for All Seasons by Robert Bolt

My 30 years of continuous service teaching in a number of primary and secondary schools, adult and youth centres, one of HM prisons, and a university department meant I taught around 25,000 timetabled lessons across a number of subject areas. Over the subsequent 20 years, in various roles home and abroad, I have visited 15,000+ lessons in over 1,000 settings.

The A–Z of Great Classrooms is a celebration of that magical double act of teaching and learning, organised around the 26 letters of the English alphabet.

I have tried to distil what happens in classrooms where learners are engaged and excited by what the skilled and knowledgeable teacher presents, and I have weaved in student voice, examples from schools, personal reflections and commentary.

In preparing this book, I asked a number of colleagues in different countries to write down words they might use by way of A–Z chapter headings. (It is fascinating to do this exercise in different cultures and reflect on nuance in language.) The lists differed a little – we each lean to our favourite words with the resonances they have for us through experience – but the essence of memorable classrooms did not differ.

Across continents I have enjoyed being in the presence of children, young people and adults being taught by teachers who love their work and whose passion for subject shines through their every gesture and every word. The best lessons – you just don't want them to end! And there's nothing quite like the professional privilege of being in such classrooms, laboratories, dance studios, workshops, music practice rooms, sports halls, libraries, learning centres, sensory zones, outdoor settings, lecture theatres – wherever the learning unfolds.

The word 'classroom' is used throughout the book to include all of these, and other learning and teaching spaces in primary, special and secondary schools. The words 'pupil', 'student' and 'child' are used interchangeably to encompass the 3–19 age range.

Virtual/blended teaching and learning came into all our lives in a significant way during the global COVID-19 pandemic – a 'clicks not bricks' era; the best features of that period have been absorbed into school, college and university blended practices. Yet I hear few students or teachers nostalgic for a diet of online learning. Evocations and images of classrooms in the flesh are what this book is all about.

In Section One, readers will form their own views about whether the A–Z alphabetical headings impose an editorial straitjacket when teaching and learning are such dynamic affairs. An extended Venn diagram or a series of linked Olympic rings might well be a richer way of presenting the complexities, intricacies and flow of classrooms. In the end, a book needs some order. Each word, from **A**rrival to **Z**oon, is a starting point, with interweaving between the headings.

The seven readings that punctuate the A–Z have been selected to bring together powerful 'other' voices on the subjects of children, teachers, learning, classrooms and the teaching profession. Section Two of the book presents further material for study and for professional development, all focused on the commerce of the classroom.

For some – maybe many – readers, there will be omissions. I'll enjoy reading that feedback in the spirit of every text being open to challenge and interpretation. Please contact me at royb88@gmail.com or www. blinks.education.

Roy Blatchford

PS Recommended reading: *The Schoolmaster* by Arthur Benson, referred to in this book. Written in an altogether different era, it captures in just 80 pages the essence of what it is to be a great teacher.

SECTION
ONE

READING 1

All of the top performing systems I visited take a similar approach to teaching, and do most or all of the following: they are selective about who enters their teacher training programmes; their teacher training programmes are hosted in respected institutions and last at least a year; they only confer teacher certification on those who... successfully pass these programmes and an induction period and they ensure teachers are mentored in their first few years and remain in close collaboration with experienced colleagues beyond that through weekly planning sessions. This means they can then give teachers autonomy to get on with their work (supported by further professional development), which makes the profession attractive, and allows the teacher training programmes to be selective. It is a professionalising cycle, and it means that teachers have the three things – mastery, autonomy and relatedness – which enhance intrinsic motivation.

Cleverlands by Lucy Crehan

ARRIVAL

From the point of view of the learners, it is surely the journey to the classroom that shapes mindset, feelings and attitudes as they enter a lesson. All schools and settings have their own bespoke routines, rightly so. Some routines are more student friendly than others and wise leaders keep these under review, listening to and acting upon children's feedback.

As a visitor to a school, I regularly ask why some schools still have harsh bells to interrupt learning and conversation when everyone has the time on their wrist or their device. Many have sensibly abandoned bells and buzzers. One school I encountered sounds a few pips to give notice that the lesson will end in five minutes, though I'm not persuaded that this is any better to help the flow of the day. Another plays soft music for five minutes to mark lesson change time, a sort of musical chairs approach which the students like – and their timekeeping is impressive.

For many years I used to say, perhaps unkindly and certainly provocatively, that there were some corridors in some secondary schools (home and abroad) where you would not want to entrust your own child. Those days are largely and happily gone. Yet it remains the case that the 'corridor experience' is not a consistently stimulating one for many students in our secondary schools.

In some places still there is a *carelessness* at work rather than a *carefulness*: lack of colour, cleanliness and character in corridors and common spaces means young people potentially arrive at lessons in quite the wrong frame of mind. In palpable contrast, at their best there are many, many corridors where the language of mathematics, geography and design shine forth from displays of students' work alongside well-chosen commercial posters that promote subject knowledge and a spirit of enquiry and scholarship.

Entering lively subject areas in secondary schools, one can encounter a welcoming display of photos of teaching staff and some well-chosen pieces of personal information about each.

Or another area welcomes with quotations from current and former students about how much they enjoyed teaching and learning in that subject domain.

Or yet another celebrates recent student achievements in the creative arts, including photos of current drama productions in rehearsal. Topicality of displays shows teachers care, and are proud of their subject and its especial contribution to the life of every student who walks in.

To move towards some classrooms is to be taken on a memorable learning journey: 'work of the week' or 'wow work' or 'outstanding achievement' attractively posted (laminated) on noticeboards celebrates what children and students have recently produced. In many primary schools with a healthy and proportionate approach to risk (don't let the caretaker say displays are a health and safety hazard!), corridors become rainforests, desert landscapes and undersea exploration zones – all in the best interests of promoting a stimulating context in which to explore new skills and knowledge.

To go that extra mile: take the primary school corridor in which Anne Frank's attic room in Amsterdam had been marked out with tape on the floor and recreated with its sparse furniture – children walked alongside it aghast that someone could live in such a small space for so long.

Or take another primary school which, studying the *Titanic*, had constructed in the corridor a life-size lifeboat modelled on those of the time of the infamous sinking – creative teachers at work to bring alive a history topic. And, in James Joyce's words, taking the *recherche biscuit*, I walked into one international school's atrium to find a Formula One car created by students with 3D printers – and could they talk about it!

Some schools have open spaces that are dynamic learning zones alongside classrooms, thereby extending the opportunities for independent and group learning (including with parents and volunteers), surrounded by further curriculum prompts and hands-on materials. Most schools harness assembly halls, dining areas and entrance halls to give the message to students that it is not only in classrooms that important learning matters.

One richly multicultural and multilingual school has the national flag of every student and staff member hanging from the ceiling of the hall, ever a powerful reminder of the 70+ nationalities in the school population. In one of the many excellent primaries I visit regularly, the headteacher declares to her colleagues: 'the corridors are my classroom walls'. Intermittently she unashamedly steals the best displays in classrooms to place in common areas that everyone sees every day, and which are vibrant celebrations of children's curriculum work.

****

In an early edition of the 'Good Schools Guide', one piece of advice to parents when choosing their child's school ran as follows. Ask yourself the question: 'when the headteacher walks around the corridors does he squash the children, or do they squash him?'

There is something in that half tongue-in-cheek question about how children and students conduct themselves on the way to lessons and what expectations are made of them by staff. Each school properly has its own ways of doing, but it is always worth observing and reflecting on how less confident young people manage lesson changes, and thus what frame of mind they are in when arriving at a lesson. In favour currently in a number of secondary schools are *silent* corridors as students move around the building: an anathema to some, desirable and workable for others.

Once at the classroom door, what greets the child or student? In the best special and primary schools I know, there are photographs on the door of the staff who work in that room, and, depending on class size, photos of all the children too. Certainly, it is a prevailing theme in successful schools that classroom doors project a basic message to students of 'welcome to this room'. And one popular poster adorning entrances to primary and secondary classrooms alike reads:

BEFORE you speak…**THINK!**

T	Is it......True?
H	Is it......Helpful?
I	Is it......Inspiring?
N	Is it......Necessary?
K	Is it......Kind?

A final point on arrival. Schools have various approaches to queueing outside rooms or students entering directly, and special, primary and secondary adopt systems that suit their architecture and context. It is clear to me, as someone who visits a number of different settings each week, that a climate of 'teaching with the door open' (literally or metaphorically) prevails in successful schools.

Outward-facing schools promote a culture of outward-facing teachers whose message to any visitor is: 'The door is open, come in and see what's going on – you'll enjoy it.' And, of course, to their colleagues they are giving a similar message: 'Come in and offer any thoughts on what I'm doing, and I'll do the same for you tomorrow. That's what this profession is all about. Everyone is interested in doing something better tomorrow than they did it today.'

ASIDE

Start a lesson with purposeful play

Stinky-pinkies

Example: a handbook about long-eared dogs

Answer: spaniel manual

1. A conceited horse rider
2. An unfeeling friend

---

3. Dubious Scottish drink
4. Clergyman's underpants
5. Summer flower disappointment

Side-by-side

Example: a small citrus fruit; touchable

Answer: tangerine; tangible

1. A structure leading out to sea; to make a hole through
2. A savoury appetiser; a hoofed quadruped with a flowing mane
3. The person in charge of a ship; an explanation appended to a picture
4. A medical listening device; a hat with a very wide brim
5. A brave woman; a wading bird with long legs

Homophones

Example: the first day – an ice-cream concoction

Answer: Sunday – sundae

1. Unmoving – paper and envelopes
2. Alcoholic drink – disapproving shouts
3. Middle of the body – unwanted material
4. Pulled along – a tailless amphibian
5. Exact – of the seashore

Russian Dolls

Example: Put a word for eternal into a sea creature to get excited

Answer: ever + fish = feverish

1. Put a group into a vegetable to make the former monetary unit of Spain
2. Put anger into a vapour to make places for cars

3. Put a heavenly creature into a board game to make a word for eternal
4. Put a personal word into an American railway to make a glossy substance
5. Put a rodent inside an insect to make a word for chastise
6. Put a pet animal into a pig's dwelling to describe a disorganised person
7. Put a taxi into a female horse to make a word for grisly

(Answers on page 205.)

BEHAVIOURS

The previous chapter opened with the assertion that the journey to the classroom shapes the mood, mindset and attitudes of students as they arrive at a lesson. A Hollywood film director once said of his cast that 80 per cent of success was turning up on time. Schools work to ensure that most children are in school most of the time, with all the serious challenges of attendance that have come about in a post-pandemic era. 'Long COVID' in education is as real as it is in health, and pupils' variable attendance is a worrying legacy.

From the moment children walk into the classroom, it is the individual teacher who picks up the 'behaviour and attitudes' torch and determines how the session will flow.

It is a truism to affirm that unless teachers are motivated, passionate, energetic, engaged and creative it is unlikely children will be. From the moment pupils enter a room – and it is likely to be a room they enter daily in primary and special schools, and a few times a week in secondary schools – their antennae sense how well organised and prepared the teacher (and support staff member) is for what lies ahead. If children sense a lack of preparedness, their attention will waver; if they sense there is something stimulating, well planned and ready to go, they will respond with alacrity.

It is the teacher's behaviours which fundamentally shape a great classroom. His or her body language, especially eye contact, needs to command the learning space; that command is physical, social and intellectual. The trope that 'teachers have eyes in the backs of their heads' is not far from the truth.

Effective teachers welcome students into the room warmly, knowing by name everyone in the group, being solicitous of collective well-being, and going the extra step (perhaps with a knowing nod) if they are aware that a particular child needs comfort and reassurance. The teachers' bright interpersonal skills set a tone that pupils feed off.

They have an eagle eye on how pupils move into the room with consideration for others; on what pupils are wearing (correcting any uniform breaches); and as they settle to their tables and get out their equipment an eye to see that everyone has what they need to start good learning. That routine underpins what will happen in the course of the lesson; when teachers secure that routine, students at once know they are in safe and capable hands. The 'I do, you do, we do' is one such deliberate approach practised by teachers and respected by pupils.

Great classrooms are places where groups of young minds come to explore ideas, learn new knowledge and skills, and push themselves to the limits of their thinking. These classrooms are places of talking and listening. When one person talks, others must listen – and listen carefully and actively. Without that mutual understanding, progress is limited. Thus, the teacher's proper insistence on the rules of engagement in his or her classroom is vital – when the expectations are clear to everyone, attitudes to learning will be excellent.

Inspection and review frameworks around the world – influenced by Ofsted – use the phrase 'behaviour and attitudes'. To my mind this phrase places the two nouns in the wrong order, and misses the better wording of 'behaviours for learning'.

Great schools in fact do not talk about behaviour and disruption. Why would they? Sensible behaviour, courtesy to others and no disruption in classrooms are a given.

In my experience as an HMI working with underperforming schools, the more leaders and teachers talk about corridor and classroom behaviour, the more they are talking themselves into a downward spiral of student misbehaviour. To be realistic, in just about any school there will be a few young people who do not find the routines and expectations of the institution easy to follow or rise to. In the true sense of the word, they are disruptors, for whatever reason. Their individual therapeutic needs must be met intelligently in the interests of the majority who find the rules and regulations acceptable, and respond accordingly.

Almost all schools have so-called behaviour policies. Where these policies have been established listening to the student voice, and where they present clarity and are commonly interpreted by all staff, then the whole school atmosphere, ethos and general sense of calm and purpose follow seamlessly. In turn, that whole-school policy underpins every classroom, and many schools have golden rules or similar displays on classroom boards about what is expected in classrooms. See pages 196–198 for one example.

It is the fair and consistent application of golden rules that is vital. In common with players in any game in sport who usually know the rules and are very quick to question the referee when the rules are in their view misapplied, so too with pupils in classrooms. With that youthful passion for things to be fair, pupils want rules to be enforced without fear or favour. Sometimes – in common with sportswomen and men – children need to learn to live with a grey rather than a black and white interpretation and judgement by their teacher. That is part of maturing.

To summarise: what teachers expect is what they will get back from those they teach. If the whole school is at ease with itself in terms of how pupils are expected to conduct themselves, and if the ground rules are shared thoughtfully and interpreted fairly, then purposeful play and learning can unfold in every classroom. And a genuine culture of kindness and mutual respect permeates.

The craft of classroom management

A few teachers fresh to the profession whom I have observed just seem to be able to walk into a classroom and start teaching effectively. They are not numerous, but they exist and often lead commentators to say that 'teachers are "born not made"'. What these and accomplished teachers practise every day is the quiet management of pupils in what seems an effortless manner.

(As a young teacher I was given the wise advice by a mentor to prepare myself for the following 'visitors' who would surely throw the pupils' concentration: a bee, the headteacher, an inspector, snow out of the window, the fire alarm, a child with an epileptic seizure in class. In my early days, each of these happened and my management was far from effortless. Happily, the child was fine.)

Watch an early years practitioner welcome a group of four-year-olds into a classroom in the morning, saying hello and goodbye to parents, then unfussily settling them on the carpet to begin their phonics work. Watch them half an hour later move to their attractive learning zones, not a minute wasted. Watch them be drawn together an hour later for a sharing of achievements session before they move – with buzz, not noise – to break-time snacks.

To take another example: watch a Year 11 history teacher welcome students who, having prepared in a previous lesson for what they are doing today, at once get into their groups of four, take out their essays and are poised to start. With the gentlest of reminders from the teacher about effective group chairing and giving space to everyone to contribute, the students immediately enter into animated and constructive discussion of the causes of the regional conflict they are studying for GCSE. Here again, there is buzz, not noise and off-task chatter.

Critically, the history teacher circulates, knowing when to listen (most of the time) and occasionally prompt with her expert knowledge. If she were to leave the room, the students wouldn't notice, the hallmark of high quality independent and collaborative learning. It looks effortless. It is the embodiment of the 10,000 hours of purposeful practice, championed by social commentator Malcolm Gladwell.

Pupils' responses

On a review of a university's English faculty, I spent many hours observing students in seminars and lecture halls. It was interesting to see, even here, 'the boys in the back row' on their phones, connecting with another world well beyond the themes of the seminar. With boys and girls alike, that habit starts young. While most pupils most of the time engage with the lesson they are in – unless it really has not been well planned – a minority of students find concentration difficult and need intervention from the teacher or perhaps a support staff member.

What is vital is that the intervention and support are timely and help the pupil feel better about themselves and the potential they have to engage and complete a set task. This is much easier said than done, and requires teachers to work out – over time and collaborating with colleagues – how best to refocus a disengaged student.

The commerce of classrooms is endlessly fascinating. Yes, there can be to-fro futility in disciplining youngsters who are wasting their own precious time and that of others. In extremis, an oft-cited reason for teachers leaving the profession is that they have been worn down by behaviour management issues. And the profession as a whole needs to take this reason very seriously.

Yet the overwhelming majority of classrooms each day provide a safe, secure and stimulating environment for enjoyable learning: safe spaces for teachers and pupils to be themselves, take risks and 'fail wisely'.

These classrooms, their expectations and routines, are created by great teachers – and pupils cannot fail to respond with head and heart to their teacher's professional craft, and the teacher's belief in them as individuals to be the best they can be. Students' self-esteem, resilience and mindset are all part of this cocktail – the best teachers do what they can to ensure that students are motivated and that their self-starters are in good working order, every day of the week, every day of the school year.

And, of course, parents and carers have a decisive role to play in every child's self-starter being in fine working order. The flourishing home–school partnership matters. Tony Little, a former headteacher, sums it up brilliantly below – a manifesto to display in every school's reception area.

ASIDE

Ten questions I would wish parents should ask of themselves if considering our school:

1. Do I believe my child is almost perfect?
2. Do I like rules and regulations until my child breaks them?

3. Am I happy gossiping about the school to anyone who will listen, but reluctant to talk to the head?

4. Do I go in at the deep end when someone criticises my child?

5. Am I an expert because I went to school myself?

If the answer to any of the above is 'yes', please find another school.

6. Am I prepared to work with the school and pull my weight?

7. Can I strike a balance between being a Velcro parent and a ghost?

8. Can I support my child and support the school through difficult times?

9. Can I suppress my frustrated ambitions and let my child be herself?

10. Will I deflect rumour and find out the facts from the school?

If the answer to any one of questions 6–10 is 'yes', welcome. We will be able to work with you and your child will flourish.

An Intelligent Person's Guide to Education by Tony Little

Q. What do you have displayed in your school reception area by way of welcome?

CRAFT

'craft' *noun*

– skill and experience, especially in relation to making objects; a job or activity that needs skill and experience, or something produced using skill and experience

The Dutch conductor Bernard Haitink (1929–2021) enjoyed a career spanning 65 years at the highest levels of music making. He was a musician ill at ease with the cult of the charismatic maestro. Yet in his time he led the London Philharmonic and the Chicago Symphony Orchestra, and was music director of Glyndebourne and Covent Garden. Unlike most of his contemporaries, he never thought of himself as interpreting music, or of wanting to do anything with it other than bring it to life.

Fellow conductor Simon Rattle observed that with Haitink 'the normal problems of ensemble or balance simply vanish. If we can't play well under Bernard, it's time to take up another profession.' Another commentator on Haitink's inspiring style noted that he knew exactly what he wanted, when to hold back, when to let go, and when simply to leave it to the players 'whose devotion to him reflected his faith in them'.

I was struck by both these observations when reflecting on the *craft* at work in every successful classroom. When one watches the best teachers in action, it is that quiet command which shines forth. And every time a decision in class comes up, the qualitatively 'correct' choice is made. The action, in itself, is nothing special; the care and consistency with which it is made *is*. Acts of intervention, challenge and support with students are for the most part *deliberate*, rooted in experience. Spontaneity, of course, always plays its part.

The most effective teaching – the professional craft of the classroom – is a many-splendoured thing, multi-faceted, with these features at the core:

- positive relationships
- meticulous planning
- skilful orchestration of time
- strong subject knowledge
- adroit modelling
- intellectual curiosity
- fascinating digression
- teachers' personal stories of learning
- illuminating questions
- humour.

These are the key elements that bring subjects and skills alive for students in classrooms, and help them remember new facts, figures, ideas and concepts. For example, watch a skilled art, music or design technology teacher, or an early years practitioner, and you see the intuitive knowing when to intervene, when to back off, when to let go which characterised Haitink's approach to the talented musicians with whom he worked across the world.

(I'm no expert on what poor conductors do, though this may resonate: less effective teaching in classrooms falls back on didactic delivery, low expectations of how students should listen carefully to one another, and a sense of drift without a solid consensus in the room of the purpose of the session.)

Further, skilled, intelligent practitioners know when to speak, when to listen, when to summarise, when to allow digression. The care and consistency with which they conduct is notable. This springs from years of practice observing others do things right and do things badly. In the same way that Haitink immersed himself as a young conductor in orchestral scores, top teachers have paid their dues as juniors, soaking up effective ways of doing from their seniors. Above all, they model and nurture strong professional relationships.

A special word on the skilful orchestration of time. In the sparkling classroom, time is very carefully managed and every minute counts. That does not mean that teachers rattle on at pace, galloping through the scheme of work and syllabus for fear of running out of time before the examination arrives. What it does mean is that confident teachers unfold narratives and explanations at a speed consistent with students' understanding and ability to internalise new concepts, knowledge and skills.

Vitally, and students always comment on this as being important for their learning, it means teachers offering moments – and more – for young minds to reflect, ponder and, yes, sit in awe and wonder, whether in the outdoor garden, the physics laboratory or the Harkness history seminar. These is a conscious design and elegance about this in great classrooms.

The accomplished teachers in command of their craft practise being excellent – and of course those they teach remember them for that and are inspired, in turn, perhaps to become teachers or lecturers themselves. The Greek philosopher Aristotle reminds us that excellence is never an accident – that it is always the result of high intention, sincere effort and intelligent execution.

High intention in practice means that teachers set out high, specific ambitions in their respective domains.

Sincere effort means that teachers approach their daily and weekly tasks with a sincerity and commitment that is personally and professionally satisfying.

Intelligent execution means that teachers think intelligently and practically about the best ways to achieve their goals. They are inspiring conductors irrespective of the subject.

****

In his memorable summary of what every lesson should contain (see page 106), Arthur Benson writes: 'Exactly in what proportion the cauldron should be mingled, and what its precise ingredients should be, must be left to the taste and tact of the teacher.'

His words are a potent reminder that no two teachers are the same. Every teacher has his or her own X factor, their unique personality which they bring to a lesson. And given no two lessons are identical, even with the same teacher and the same group of students, the craft of the classroom involves adjusting content to the hour, to the day. As Shakespeare attested in *Hamlet*, 'let your own discretion be your tutor'.

On inspection, I once observed an excellent music teacher (and pianist) with a class of nine-year-olds. I had on my schedule to visit for 20 minutes. I stayed for the hour. I didn't want to leave, such was the quality of the teaching. At the start she said to the class: 'We're going to cover three notes today.' Fifteen minutes later, she said: 'I think we'll cover two notes today.' Fifteen minutes after that she said warmly to the class: 'Let's make sure we cover one note in depth today.' She was adjusting teaching and learning adroitly to the children in front of her, notably without fear or favour towards the inspector. Knowing when to pause and stop… is as important as starting.

Reflecting on the intricacies, complexities and 'flow' of great classrooms, in the end it is the individuality of the teacher that never goes away, just as the individual demands of every student in a class never subside. As the jocular, affectionate one-liner runs: 'Old teachers never die – they just lose their class.'

ASIDE

One primary school's set of questions about the quality of classroom life

- Does the teacher know the prior knowledge of the children? Are pupils' learning records up to date and are they influencing planning and teaching?
- What is the quality of the pupils' experience in class? Demanding, meaningful, worth doing?
- Are pupils on task and with work matched well to their ability?
- Can the pupils tell what they are doing and why they are doing it?

- Can the teacher say why pupils are doing what they are doing, and where the task is leading?
- What is the end product of the activity? What is the teacher going to do with the end product?
- What is the quality of the teacher's interventions? Sensitive? Useful?
- Does the teacher move around the class and have an eye on all learners?
- How does the teacher assess, and what do the children understand by 'assessment'?
- Does the lesson end with a round-up and reflection on what has been learned?

Q. Which of these questions are the most important to your way of looking at classrooms?

DIFFERENTIATION

Working with a group of teachers in New York on one occasion, I mentioned the word 'differentiation'. One of them said, 'Ah you mean putting students in different rooms.' In a teacher training college I visited in Mumbai the concept of separating out children by ability was an anathema, an offence to Mahatma Gandhi's founding principles.

Differentiation is certainly a culturally loaded word and one which prompts a rich array of opinion, nay prejudice, from teachers on the vocabulary of banding, setting, mixed ability, streaming, mastery and the like. The word further leads to animated discussion in staffrooms about workload when teachers are expected to create countless, subtly different worksheets, differentiated PowerPoint slides and colour-coded tasks to show they are meeting all abilities.

My other observation on this 'wicked' word in teaching and learning is rooted in an inspector visiting my lesson and telling me, as we both circulated around the room, that I had not differentiated sufficiently for a group of higher attainers. Bravely, and half-jokingly, I quickly asked whether he'd like to take over and show me how – he declined, rather po-faced. It is too easy – and simplistic – for reviewers and inspectors to criticise teachers for lack of differentiation. In a class of 10, 20, 30 students, it is just about the hardest thing any teacher has to do, in any subject and in any context.

And think for a moment of a class you have attended as an adult, maybe to learn bookkeeping, cooking, Spanish or kayaking. How many were in the class? How did the tutor differentiate her input? How did the tutor support the slow learner and extend the speedy learner? Did you think your individual learning needs were being met? There really are no easy answers.

Some assertions to start with.

Firstly, it is surely incontestable that not only what we teach but how we teach can make a great difference to children and students: whether by precept, example or demeanour, teachers exert a moral influence, for better or worse. A former HMI quotes the RE teacher who went around the class saying 'Remember God is Love' while striking the pupils on the head with a Bible.

Secondly, any selection of teaching methods or learning approaches makes its own value assumptions and by implication transmits these. It is easy to see this if one studies how the aim of unquestioned or unquestioning indoctrination is best achieved through certain highly structured and authoritarian teaching methods, including a heavy dose of rote learning. Open questions would be plainly counterproductive.

Conversely, learning by enquiry is likely to imply a commitment to following truth wherever it may be found, to basing actions on evidence and exploration, to a willingness to doubt, test and evaluate independently. Use of practical methods is based on a recognition that often we learn best by doing – an old truth, and often a true one.

Thirdly, the whole way in which learning is organised and managed in classrooms rests on fundamental educational beliefs about the learner and the learning process. It is for this reason, in effect, that people such as inspectors bang on endlessly about differentiation.

It is not just that doing things differently for different people relieves tedium and is more efficient as a means of instruction. Above all, it is the fact that the key moral value is that each member of the class is an individual with her or his own rights, character, disposition to learning and level of understanding.

All teachers know that expectations matter profoundly. What you expect from children you will surely receive. If expectations of pupils are low, then little will be achieved. When expectations are high, both the teacher and the learner surprise themselves. It is as simple and complex as that.

****

Skilful and meaningful differentiation is fundamentally rooted in the *richness* of the task or activity that a teacher sets. That richness comes from the teacher's own knowledge of how children learn and from their specialist subject matter. The studious planning of how that knowledge will be shared with the learner is decisive, scaffolding new ideas and concepts with a keen awareness of audience; teachers who differentiate successfully really *know* their students' personal learning styles and prior knowledge.

The richness of a task is as equally relevant in an early years setting as it is in an A level physics seminar. If that task is the key planned input, the skilled teacher has a fair idea of where the learning will go and how she might need to intervene, and at what point for different learners. Students offering feedback regularly comment that their teacher needs to give them more time to pause and think and understand; measured differentiation does just that in a great classroom.

It is currently fashionable to talk about 'differentiating down', and that approach clearly has merit in terms of raising expectations for all learners – the Aside below revisits that idea. But it is worth focusing especial attention on (a) what we provide for those students with special educational needs, and (b) what we mean by 'working at great depth'.

A note on special educational needs

A number of approaches are adopted in great classrooms, within a school's overall approach and attitude to inclusion. The following are worth reflecting upon.

Differentiating instruction. Special schools in particular will have children and students with a variety of different abilities and needs in every classroom, so tailoring instructions to meet those needs is vital.

Collaborative learning. Using group activities or peer work can help children learn from each other, and support opportunities in a safe and structured environment.

Visual aids. Using images, videos, graphic organisers, illustrations and other visual elements can be beneficial to understanding in depth.

Experiential learning. Activities such as field trips, hands-on practicals, and simulations can help engage students in their learning, and help them retain information.

Multi-sensory instruction. This incorporates speech, movement, visuals, and other elements to make learning more memorable and engaging.

Flexible instruction. Providing opportunities to students to complete assignments at their own pace and in the way that works best for their learning style can help engagement and understanding.

Positive reinforcement. Praise, rewards, and warm verbal and facial feedback all help motivate children and reinforce desired behaviours and attitudes to learning.

What do we mean by children working at greater depth?

If we think of 'greater depth' simply as a data measurement, we lower expectations. If we think of 'greater depth' as a way of working, we may surprise ourselves as teachers at just how many students are capable of being 'greater depth' poets, geographers, biologists, historians.

Working at greater depth means children work independently, applying what they have learned in one area of a subject to others. They apply their knowledge consistently, confidently and fluently. They are able to explain to others what they have been doing, including teaching other children what they have learned.

Take this example from the early years, which also warmly challenges preconceptions we may have about a child's apparent abilities.

Jamie is a four-year-old with delayed speech and language who consequently has had lower self-esteem and a reluctance to talk. Recently he has shown a real interest in drawing and model making. With the support of staff he has mastered tools such as scissors and hole punches and is now proficient at creating robots by attaching several different shaped pieces of paper together.

Other children are now showing an interest in making robots 'like Jamie', so we have started saying to Jamie: 'Please can you show...how you made your robot.' He has risen to this challenge and will help other children find the required resources, and model and support them with drawing and cutting. He is consequently chattier as he talks about his creations and has increased confidence as he develops relationships with his peers.

Differentiation remains a wicked word in professional discussions about classroom practice, and that will not change as long as more than one student turns up for a lesson – any lesson. Suffice to say that teachers continue to experiment, re-evaluate, push new boundaries and learn best practices from one another to meet that aspiration of a well-differentiated lesson. And when you watch someone achieving that success, don't hesitate to applaud!

ASIDE

Tips for differentiation – one school's list

- Knowing pupils' prior attainment and prior knowledge of a subject
- Meticulous tracking of pupils' progress in different skills
- Thinking through which pupils work best with others, and the optimum size for group work
- Judging when independent learning will best deepen knowledge and understanding
- Knowing when best to harness the library, film, internet to expand pupils' thinking
- Setting up one-to-one catch-up and intervention sessions before, during and after school
- Setting meaningful homework, well scaffolded for individual needs
- Knowing which factors inhibit progress, seeking to remove those barriers promptly
- Identifying special needs such as poor hand–eye coordination, delayed cognitive development, temporary medical problems
- Practising 'differentiation up and down' to ensure lower, middle and higher attainers are extended in their learning.

Q. What works well for you in class, and with different groups of pupils?

READING 2

And you called yourself a teacher?

I didn't call myself anything. I was more than a teacher. And less. In the high school classroom you are a drill sergeant, a rabbi, a shoulder to cry on, a disciplinarian, a singer, a low-level scholar, a clerk, a referee, a clown, a counsellor, a dress-code enforcer, a conductor, an apologist, a philosopher, a collaborator, a tap dancer, a politician, a therapist, a fool, a traffic cop, a priest, a mother-father-brother-sister-uncle-aunt, a bookkeeper, a critic, a psychologist, the last straw.

Teacher Man by Frank McCourt

ENVIRONMENT

Architects and designers shape lives. Look around you, whether at home, at work or at leisure. The spaces in which we live, work and play matter to our well-being and our sense of purpose and, in a professional context, make a tangible difference to the quality of our endeavours and the fulfilment we experience and value.

It is true that the venerable double act of teaching and learning can take place anywhere – and *does* if you ponder for a moment on settings, schools, colleges and universities around the world.

For many in developing countries this can mean literally gathering students under a tree or a makeshift tarpaulin or on a boat that tours islands; in some of the top international universities the spaces for learning are *Avatar* dream-like in dimension and experience. Within that vast range lie most schools in the UK, coming in all shapes and sizes. No one would underestimate some of the tired and ageing educational estate across this country that contrasts strikingly with many of the superb newer builds of the past two decades.

For the purposes of this chapter, I'll use the word 'smart' to describe great classrooms, a word a group of 11-year-olds used with obvious pride to describe their own classroom to me.

The learning environment matters, and matters at a fundamental level, whether learning is with a class of 5- or 15-year-olds. Start with the question: is it spacious enough to facilitate the demands of the contemporary curriculum? Is it light and airy? Is it at a temperature conducive to effective learning and teaching, bearing in mind teachers are usually moving around while pupils are sitting still? In some countries the ancient fan or the noisy air conditioning drowns out any voices; but turn off the fan and you boil!

Then look at how furniture is configured, probably *the* critical aspect of a classroom in shaping whether some, many or all pupils are engaged. Some teachers choose to have a desk or a table at the front on which they can spread out their planning and which provides a quiet space in which to work with individual children. Some choose to have pupils individually seated, some seated in pairs, others in groups of four; show me a group of more than four and I'll regularly observe less than good progress round that table.

A good number of teachers make very effective use of horseshoes of tables, while others, especially at senior level, harness versions of the Harkness oval table to maximise deep and creative thinking. In the best advanced level chemistry laboratory, it feels like a university seminar where collaboration and animated learning prevail to great effect.

Some schools prefer furniture to be circular, some prefer soft seating, some prefer square tables – what matters is what staff and students say works well for them. There are no orthodoxies here, but orthodoxies like sitting on the carpet for far too long in primary classes need to be questioned. Or similarly in modern foreign languages lessons where students sit in rows and practise a language to the backs of one other's heads – plain daft!

And where the whiteboard/smartboard is positioned matters too; do all children have a clear line of sight to this and any other key information that the teacher presents and that underpins good progress in the lesson? If 'command vocabulary' is a feature of every geography or science lesson, is that vocabulary readable at a distance for every student?

A regular experience for me, especially in primary schools, is to ask a couple of children to 'talk me round the room' – to describe the purpose of the various displays in their room and what they have learned though the displays. Such conversations are usually rich in dialogue and illuminating: their deep, animated knowledge linked to a particular display tells you at once how well taught that topic has been. Some settings have 'awe and wonder' or 'values' tables upon which children display personal items important to them, and which then become a focus for whole-class spiritual reflection time.

The smart classroom is also a place where what is on the walls, floor and ceiling matters. The teacher has given thought to learning prompts, keywords, photos taken by students celebrating work in progress and final outcomes, displays of high-quality pupils' work to which their peers can aspire – and how all these contribute to a climate that expects top achievement. It is striking also how in successful schools there is a consistency – not sameness – when moving from classroom to classroom and in the deliberate and careful way certain whole-school information (core values, classroom expectations, safeguarding and fire procedures) is displayed.

It is worth recording here that in some special and secondary schools there can be a deliberate practice to leave some walls bare so as not to provide distractions for pupils' attention in lessons. Displays are reserved for the rear wall only, where wandering eyes won't easily roam. One size does not fit all.

Further, the smart classroom is where book and technological resources are accessible and fit for purpose. The electronic device is present, no more nor less than a pair of scissors. It is a tool for learning which each generation of young people masters more skilfully than its predecessors. Just wonder for a moment at what primary children are doing today with Google Classroom to enhance their studies. 'Please bring me your work to talk about,' I say; they arrive with books, portfolios and invariably the portable device.

And let us not forget the many other arenas that accommodate great learning: workshops, sports halls, laboratories, drama and art and music studios – how are they configured to maximise learning and promote the knowledge and scholarship of their particular subject? The same points about light, air, acoustics, colour and furniture arrangement apply. To walk into an A level art or drama space is often to be transported to an art gallery or theatre, such are the ambience, visuals and performance quality on show from students.

Peer also into the best early years classrooms to see how the 'indoors tumbles outdoors, and the out tumbles in' related to rich curriculum content. Look at how zones for learning are cleverly set out to give formative minds the opportunity to explore the five senses. Admire how ingenious teachers and support staff are in there, foraging for materials and drapes and unusual objects. Look too at the profile of language and shape and number at every turn, and whether in every classroom there are photos of children in action displayed at a height the children can see.

When visiting nursery and Reception classes and outdoor spaces, walk on your knees and view the curated learning environment as young children see it. Ask yourself: is it an engaging space? Look around: does the environment appeal to the five senses? If I'm a kinaesthetic learner, what's here for me?

A note on adaptations for special needs. It is a distinctive feature of smart classrooms how seamlessly they accommodate children and students who have particular physical needs, making generous and appropriate space for wheelchairs or for additional technologies. Teachers in those classrooms have thought intelligently about how students are best positioned in relation to the light, the whiteboard and key learning aids. Often a fellow pupil will have been assigned to ensure that learning flows as readily for the child with identified special needs as it does for everyone else.

Finally, step inside some of the designated 'classrooms of the future' which I have come across in some of the top international schools, and which are increasingly emerging in the UK. 'Sustainability' is the watchword in their design in terms of heat and light and consumables.

One principal avowed in opening a new 3–18 school that there would be no square tables, as they belonged to the 19th and 20th centuries. Rather, all furniture should be curved and flexible, if not quite on wheels! True to intent, almost all classrooms have students studying and collaborating at circular tables, with attractive, curved soft-seating areas adjacent – and, of course, students can write on just about any surface from tables to walls, alongside their ubiquitous iPads and the 3D printers.

This chapter began with asserting the importance of securing the right environment for high-quality learning. My experience in contrasting contexts is that bright teachers have a very keen eye for such quality, ever creative and enterprising in making the best of whatever space they find themselves occupying. This is about shaping a space for those they teach. Yet let it not be forgotten that self-preservation is equally critical: if you are occupying a classroom for 190 days a year, you want it to be conducive to your own well-being and indeed to be a projection of your own personality.

Coda. I say to headteachers, with a twinkle in my eye, that every classroom should have: a water dispenser for the students; a Nespresso machine or Teasmade for the teacher; and a chaise longue at the back of the room so that, just occasionally, the teacher can actually or metaphorically recline – and watch pupils working harder than she or he is.

ASIDE

One secondary school's 'Great Expectations'

Every classroom should display

- health, safety and well-being information
- the school's five core values
- the seven habits of highly effective learners
- tutor group notices
- words of the week.

Every classroom should promote

- visual excitement in the subject
- the subject 'in the news'
- keywords and command vocabulary
- examples of students' work
- examples of 'beautiful work'.

Q. What 'classroom expectations' does your school promote?

FUN

It is a truism that what knowing parents give to their children is, in equal and balanced measure, roots and wings. So with teachers: they provide for learners the activities and experiences that provide the roots and wings of learning. An education lets you do things you couldn't do beforehand.

In what I term 'sparkling classrooms', there exists that judicious balance of the *fun and fundamentals* of learning. Fun, humour and warm relationships abound. So too does an unequivocal focus on practising basic and higher order skills. Great teachers accept no substitute.

The sparkling classroom provides a climate for learning that engenders confidence and motivation amongst the learners. It is one in which, critically, there is no fear of failure because the teacher and fellow pupils alike support one another's little triumphs and disasters. Opportunities for risk-taking, exploration of new knowledge and concepts, and experimentation permeate. Learners' potential is spotted and encouraged. In the true sense of the word, education – 'to lead out' – underpins the learning environment.

The founder of the BBC, Lord Reith, created what are termed the 'Reithian principles', which are recognised as the BBC's mission and are principles embedded in its Royal Charter. He declared that the broadcaster should, in this order, *inform, educate and entertain*. In fact, he further stipulated that the BBC should be protected from commercial pressures, serve the whole nation, be under the control of a unified body, and be a monopoly.

One can reflect on the extent to which those same principles – a century on from the creation of the BBC in 1922 – apply in a nuanced way to schools, even to this day. Certainly, the mission to inform, educate and entertain underpins great classrooms. The skilled teacher, on a daily basis, informs and educates students, and whilst teachers are not on a mission to 'entertain' (not a word one sees as a rule in school prospectuses), a key part of the teacher's armoury is humour, wit and the common sense not to take things too seriously.

The BBC as the national broadcaster has in many ways been an arbiter of taste and tolerance down the decades, often controversially. Schools are no different. They are mirrors of the era in which they operate; they help shape attitudes and aspirations among young people; they play a pivotal role in determining each generation's attitudes and social norms.

The term 'political correctness' has its roots in Marxist-Leninist vocabulary following the Russian Revolution in 1917. It has been harnessed variously by different political groupings ever since. Today we are said by commentators to live in a 'politically correct' age.

It is certainly the case that in schools dealing with young people every day, one person's regular banter and jokes are sometimes a cause for another student to take offence. Skilled teachers make sure appropriate lines are drawn in classrooms and, indeed, where inappropriate humour is overheard in common spaces, staff are rightly quick to address it promptly with children of whatever age. Developing good social habits – and sensitivity towards the feelings of others and choice of language – starts young.

When children arrive in great classrooms there is something in the air that encourages them to relax and feel secure: this is a place where 'we can speak our minds', 'we are sensitive to others', and 'we know that it doesn't matter if we make a mistake, as we won't be laughed at' – phrases students often share when asked what they value about being in the presence of a skilled teacher.

This relaxed yet purposeful culture is created by the teacher who is comfortable in his or her own skin and is especially skilled in balancing their own professionalism with their personality and personal interests. The best teachers remain children at heart, all the days that they teach. They recount relevant tales to pupils about how they learned at school and college, and found things easy or difficult. Look around yourself in any school and this will be true. Teachers come into the profession because they like working with young people; they soon leave – or should leave – if they do not.

Early careers teachers often find balancing the professional and the personal quite difficult – overheard in staffroom: 'He's too matey with those Year 7s.' Well mentored, those teachers learn quickly about professional distance and suitable body and verbal language that strike a healthy balance.

Accomplished teachers know too that they have a legal duty to present information in a balanced way, much like the BBC, though what is 'balance' in one era may change in another period in time. Thus teachers, whether they like it or not, are role models, leading arbiters in society of what might be judged appropriate or inappropriate. A teacher of history or biology or geography, as they share their passion for subject, needs always to be careful not to slip into any form of bias or propaganda, though arguably any form of teaching 'loads the dice', as the unique personality and opinions of the teacher are part of every great classroom.

The 'relaxed but fair' ethos in a great classroom which children say they value has an undercurrent of light humour, not all of the time, but certainly no learning session passes without a smile or two on everyone's face. Teachers set the tone, sometimes with a light-hearted reference to the weather, something in the national news, an event in the school's calendar, a palindromic date, a pupil's birthday.

Frequently, humour and wit surface in the commerce of the classroom. The teacher inadvertently twists her words and comes out with something the children find funny – she at once capitalises on that moment and makes a learning point out of it. In haste, the teacher spells something incorrectly or divides two numbers wrongly on the board, promptly spots the error, smiles and turns to the pupils for them to make the corrections.

In senior classrooms, there is often wit and laughter in abundance as students read plays and texts, study sources, reflect on an experiment in the chemistry laboratory giving off toxic odours, or watch video recordings. Skilfully channelled by the teacher, the laughter 'with' and not 'at' becomes a way of embedding a new concept and can even turn into a mnemonic. When students harness wit, humour, laughter – almost taking on the role of the teacher and leading the learning – you know you are in a great classroom.

I often visit A level and IB seminar rooms and it is a particular pleasure to see students seated as a group and, for a moment, you are not quite sure who or where the teacher is because a pair of students are standing at the front conducting the learning. Invariably, whatever the topic, they will use humour to put across to their peers a particular sequence of ideas or deep thinking or mathematical trails – a sure sign that their teacher encourages this style of learning to help embed knowledge and enable students to recall it for examinations.

It is the *fun and fundamentals* of learning that deliciously come together in classrooms full of humour.

Learning has to be fun, but in the end it is about grasping the fundamentals of a particular topic. The wise teacher of Spanish says to her class that for every fun hour we do in class learning new vocabulary through song, recitation and watching the news, the students must do a 'companion hour' at home, learning by heart those new words and phrases – that is fundamental and non-negotiable if they want to make progress and attain well in the subject. The great double act of teaching and learning is crystallised in this unwritten but clear contract between teacher and pupil.

ASIDE

A little general knowledge quiz

1. How long did the Hundred Years War last?
2. Which country makes Panama hats?
3. From which animal do we get cat gut?
4. In which month do Russians celebrate the October Revolution?
5. What is a camel-hair brush made of?
6. The Canary Islands in the Pacific are named after which animal?

7. What was King George VI's first name?
8. What colour is a purple finch?
9. Where are Chinese gooseberries from?
10. What is the colour of the black box in a commercial airplane?

(Answers on page 205.)

GLOBE

One evening as a headteacher I was presenting my termly report to governors which included a section on the curriculum in schools past, present and future. I was mid presentation when one of the governors gently interrupted with words to the chair: 'I think there's only one subject worth studying on the curriculum – and it's biology'.

The words came from Dr Jane Mellanby, a distinguished Oxford University human scientist and a pioneer in widening access to the colleges. And she went on to argue brilliantly and in her characteristically authoritative style how *all* human knowledge could be taught in a biology lesson.

What ensued was one of the most fascinating discussions I have ever been party to around a table of school governors, as each chipped in with their thoughts on the taught subjects that really matter. Naturally, they called upon memories of school, but also reflected on the demands of contemporary society. As in any great lesson, it was a digression that could not have been planned for, but which was treasured by everyone present. The chair of governors let conversation flow for a while, then, in his usual consummate style, ably summed up, uniting all differences, and passed back to the headteacher to continue his report.

So much for biology. Let's turn to an executive headteacher who oversees seven primary schools in inner London where pupils' attainment is outstanding. As a federation, the seven schools are very similarly organised, with high expectations of all learners and excellent curriculum planning led by a core team of teachers.

That team's core belief is that everything can be taught through the globe. To that end, every school reception area and every classroom contains a globe – not just *any* globe, but an elaborate, all-singing, all-dancing model, to be found in all good catalogues. They have crystal-clear design and are large, illuminated and highly coloured, with physical and human geographical features – and they are loved by the children, who find them irresistible to touch and whirl. The schools offer an exceptional primary education where, among a number of distinctive features, geography as a subject sings – not always the case in primary schools.

It is my contention too that every classroom should have, front and centre, a globe, whether in special, primary or secondary. First, the globe is an ever-present reminder to children that they are part of a global community and that when they leave school they will be global citizens shaping an international future. The globe provides a wonderful teaching resource, an everyday object to which to refer, taking learning out of the classroom and relating it to daily news and the real world. (I concede that a large map of the world on the wall might be a fallback in every secondary classroom.)

In classrooms I enter in different countries, I often ask pupils: 'Who in the room has a family member living in a different time zone, and would they ring them at this moment?' What ensues is invariably an illuminating exchange as pupils (and often the teachers) discover where their families have come from and whether indeed a phone call would be welcomed at that particular moment. It is a reminder, if one were needed, of the cultural diversity of the contemporary classroom.

One might argue whether biology has the edge over geography were there to be a sole subject taught in school classrooms – a debate for the staffroom. When I posed that question about the most important subject on the curriculum to one group of Year 8s, they told me that geography was common sense, they didn't need French, history didn't matter, and only English and mathematics were important to them. It is a fruitful debate to have with pupils of any age.

Students today of all ages have a keen awareness of climate change, sustainability, environmental degradation and all matters relating to the future of their planet. Senior students in Europe have a strong grasp of the concept of a continent without borders and the challenges of mass migration from the global South to the global North, especially as increased temperatures render parts of Africa uninhabitable. They are inspired by studying these topics. As a result, many schools have now adopted aspects of the United Nations Sustainable Development Goals into their formal and informal curriculum.

UN Sustainable Development Goals

1. No poverty
2. Zero hunger
3. Good health and well-being
4. Quality education
5. Gender equality
6. Clean water and sanitation
7. Affordable and clean energy
8. Decent work and economic growth
9. Industry, innovation and infrastructure
10. Reduced inequalities
11. Sustainable cities and communities
12. Responsible consumption and production
13. Climate action
14. Life below water
15. Life on land
16. Peace, justice and strong institutions
17. Partnerships for the goals.

At one level, this is an ambitious wish list for a perfect world; on another, it provides an excellent platform for formal study with rich cross-curricular links. What is certainly true is that students of all ages are highly motivated by schemes of work that touch on the issues above and that have such potent relevance to their lives now and in the future. It is the case that the average child born today will live well into the 22nd century – a sobering fact as the world's population is projected to peak at 9.7 billion in 2064.

The great classrooms of today and tomorrow have a moral and social imperative to ensure that the current generation in our schools 'looks up and outwards' to appreciate the global context they inhabit. Eco-capital walks alongside cultural capital. Informed teachers make a point of relating learning – whether physics, geography, design or food nutrition – to the wider world and sustainability issues. Certainly, the best lessons include well-planned moments looking out of the window for a purpose, literally or metaphorically.

You see similar in early years classes where a blow-up plastic globe is passed around a group and they are asked to estimate how much of the world is sea or land. Young children find 'holding the world in their hands' a fascinating notion. You see that same global appreciation in PSHE lessons, with animated conversations about equality and education being unevenly distributed in different cultures. You see it too in IB individuals and societies courses, where senior students are debating the carbon footprint of invisible and visible exports.

And you see it powerfully in this line, posted above a science teacher's desk: 'There are more micro-plastics in our seas than stars in the galaxy.'

In the famous novel *To Kill A Mockingbird* by Harper Lee, lawyer Atticus Finch offers advice to his daughter, Scout: 'You never really understand a person until you consider things from his point of view…until you climb into his skin and walk around in it.' The great classroom of today, connected digitally as it is with so many other classrooms, is underpinned by a sense of young people in that room being global citizens who will live in and shape tomorrow's world.

A note on students with English as an additional language (EAL)

It seems appropriate here in the context of the globe to mention the many students in our schools who have the added richness in their lives of speaking a second, third or even fourth language.

Depending on their levels of fluency in English, schools arrange additional classes and/or in-class provision to support these learners. What is a hallmark of great classrooms is the way in which teachers (a) make a point of ensuring EAL students are assisted with absorbing and using subject specialist command vocabulary and keywords; (b) harness the linguistic diversity so that children share vocabulary from their different languages with fellow pupils.

It might be unfair, nay provocative, to assert that the de facto world language being English makes UK students rather lazy towards other languages. Great classrooms counter that attitude and celebrate linguistic diversity, seizing opportunities even and especially where most pupils are monolingual English speaking.

Coda. As the 2020s become the 2030s and 2040s, what can appear today as distant climate goals will press in upon the human condition. Each successive generation of the world's schoolchildren will impress upon their teachers the existential importance of a changing climate. Very few schools today have not adopted targets and actions related to their sustainable future, with all the complexities that brings. The 'globe in our hands' promises to be a potent image in every classroom.

ASIDE

A Year 11 history class were given the following, and asked to order them in terms of which they felt were the most important in determining the West's power globally, and how these are changing today.

The West developed six killer applications that the Rest lacked

Competition, in that Europe itself was politically fragmented and that within each monarchy or republic there were multiple competing corporate entities.

The Scientific Revolution, in that all the major 17th century breakthroughs in mathematics, physics, chemistry and biology happened in Western Europe.

The rule of law and representative government, in that an optimal system of social and political order emerged in the English-speaking world, based on private property rights and the representation of property owners in elected legislatures.

Modern medicine, in that nearly all the major 19th and 20th century breakthroughs in healthcare, including the control of tropical diseases, were made by Western Europeans and North Americans.

The consumer society, in that the Industrial Revolution took place where there was both a supply of productivity-enhancing technologies and a demand for more, better, and cheaper goods, beginning with cotton garments.

The work ethic, in that Westerners were the first people in the world to combine more extensive and intensive labour with higher savings rates, permitting sustained capital accumulation.

(after Niall Ferguson in *Civilization*)

HOMEWORK

Conduct a poll amongst children, parents and teachers on the subject of 'homework' – as many schools regularly do – and you'll receive a diverse range of responses. These range from, perhaps predictably, children asking why they have to work at home as well as at school, parents welcoming further study being set, and teachers questioning its value. The debate ensues, with AI technologies popping up increasingly in the conversations.

In great classrooms teachers have a clarity of vision about the purpose and impact of homework, often rooted in years of trial and error. They see its purpose as expecting pupils, outside of the classroom:

1. to follow up a particular topic under study in order to consolidate understanding
2. to build further on what they have learned and extend understanding
3. to help establish the independent study habit when beyond the gaze of the teacher.

Great classrooms fit within a whole-school shared expectation about the value and importance of homework; for students who are unable to work at home, the school provides space on site for pupils to work in a supervised and attractive environment such as the library or learning resource centre, which is conducive to private study. To this day it is still called 'Supervised prep' in some schools.

The pandemic-induced era of home, virtual and blended learning for students across the world redefined the word 'homework', and made all parties look afresh at the place of learning at home by way of extension to what is taught in classrooms. Parents gazed literally into classrooms like never before and learned anew alongside their children.

Schools are places of historic routine and to a large extent 'the old normal' has resumed. But what we mean by 'homework' has been looked at afresh. A small minority of schools have taken a principled position that the 190 days a year in school provide sufficient time to cover the required curriculum, and thus no homework is set for pupils. Independent learning at home is a matter of choice.

The majority of schools have reshaped their homework policies, ditched what was not effective and refreshed what in many cases were tired practices. In so doing, their focus has been on the impact of homework on improving the whole-school curriculum experience for all pupils.

In the early years of primary education, homework has historically been light touch and focused on setting a few fun practical activities which parents can do with their children at home, with a particular focus on language development. Kitchen chemistry with its opportunities to weigh and measure; art and craft with the scope to mix colours, sew materials, design artefacts; garden activities to provide opportunities for children to work outside, get their hands dirty and learn a little about the natural world – all these complement the school curriculum.

For most primary practitioners, the value of regular homework lies first and foremost in promoting the independent reading habit through ensuring that children read regularly at home and enjoy books with their families. The reading diary has been an unmistakable feature of primary education for decades. Further, in the upper years of primary, homework that reinforces classwork in mathematics and science is commonplace, alongside research for humanities topics and design projects being covered in the curriculum.

In special schools it is striking how in great classrooms homework, rooted in the planned curriculum, is curated carefully, with the intention of pupils sharing with their families the small steps they have achieved in school. Activities are set to encourage pupils to practise at home a new skill they have learned, with the emphasis on transferability of skills.

The balance of academic and applied learning characterises best practice in secondary classrooms. That is to say that much homework is about students reinforcing through reading and written exercises new knowledge they have acquired in class. It is also about applying those newly acquired skills and knowledge to rich extension tasks which deepen understanding. For students in the examination years, there is no escaping the mantra that for every hour spent in the classroom, there is an hour of independent study to match what the teacher has presented – and triple that when it comes to the demands of Year 11 and sixth form study.

The above is about the *what*. But it is the *how* that matters equally – *how* in a great classroom homework is set.

Skilled teachers know that for homework to be valued by pupils they have to see it as relevant, engaging, worth giving time to (competing with leisure pursuits), and integral to the programme of work. Accordingly, homework is threaded adeptly into the fabric of the lesson: previous homeworks are referred to and recalled, and the next homework arises naturally from the lesson content. In great classrooms you rarely see the teacher suddenly rush to set homework at the end of the lesson as though they have just remembered 'it's French homework today on the timetable'.

Talking to pupils, it is clear that they value (sometimes affectionately curse!) homework which they consider the teacher has thought about carefully beforehand and which will genuinely help them consolidate their understanding of a topic. This might be focused wider reading, researching a subject to present in class the following day, or a follow-up written assignment.

The one point students invariably make when it comes to written homework is: in great classrooms it is marked *promptly*, with formative comments on how to improve the next homework piece. In the words of one sixth-former: 'I always hand in study assignments on time because I know they'll be marked and given back to me within a week.'

By common consent, the era of virtual and blended learning triggered a quiet revolution in how teachers and students harnessed digital and online learning, from Teams and Zoom to Google Classroom and YouTube. Yet it remains a feature of our education system – in need of urgent reform – that students still have to turn up on the days of national tests and examinations and *write* with a pen.

Thus teachers continue to set homework that reinforces the importance of writing. Equally, students relish the opportunities that teachers give them to explore the internet, video, and social media as an aspect of home study. Further advances in communication and other technologies will only serve to extend those opportunities.

Homework as we know it has been part of 'the old normal' in schools for generations. There was a time when the scrappy written note from a parent to say 'Kavita didn't know what the homework was so she hasn't completed it' was commonplace. It is in text form today. Yet no student has the excuse of not knowing what homework has been set, as it is sure to be on the school's intranet.

Whether 'homework' as we recognise it today survives another generation of children going through the school system, time and generative AI will no doubt tell us.

ASIDE

Ideas for having fun with maths at home

Early years

- Number spotting. Number recognition. Doors, buses, prices — call out every time you see a number in the street and the shops.
- Number treasure hunt. Hide numbers around the house for children to find and name. Count up all the numbers.
- Towers. Make them out of plastic cups or play bricks. Count them and compete to make the tallest tower.
- Sing number songs like 'Five little speckled frogs'.

5–7 years

- Make up simple little calculations together. You sometimes get the answer wrong. Let your child tell you what you did wrong.
- Learn-by-heart songs with numbers in them like 'Hickory Dickory Dock'.

- Count forwards and backwards within 20, from any starting point, then try with 100. See how fast you can do this with a child, staying accurate. Try with just counting even numbers and odd numbers.
- Encourage learning to tell the time accurately by making reference to time at key points in the day: 'It's 6 o'clock, time for dinner'.

8–11 years

- Practise and play games to help memorise times tables to 12×12, and their corresponding division facts.
- Practise and memorise number bonds to 10, 20, 100, 1,000.
- Play card games like whist and cribbage, which are great for mental arithmetic. Darts are even better – play safely!
- Play board games together that involve logic and reasoning skills.

Alumnis Trust

Q. What does your school produce to support learning at home which you and families find of real value?

READING 3

As part of my work I sometimes follow a class or group of pupils for a whole day to try to capture how the school day appears to pupils. At the end of the day I tried to summarise their response to their schooling.

There had been no hostile rebellion from them, though they had been rebuked many times for 'talking' and for not paying attention. School lessons for them appeared to be like seven very dull television programmes, which could not be switched off. They did not want to watch and made little effort to do so; occasionally the volume rose to a very high level, so they listened; occasionally the programme became sufficiently interesting to command their attention, but it was never more than a momentary diversion from the general monotony.

Part of the problem appeared to be that they were not, in fact, seven new independent programmes. All of them were serials, which demanded some knowledge of earlier episodes. Indeed, most of the teachers generously provided a recapitulation of earlier episodes at the beginning of every lesson. But the girls had lost track of the story long ago. Two of the programmes were, in fact, repeats; since their first broadcast had aroused no interest in the girls, it is not surprising that the repeat evoked no new response.

So these two girls responded as most of us do when faced with broadcasts of low quality that we cannot switch off: they talked through the broadcast whenever they could. The easiest form of resistance was to treat the lessons as background noise which from time to time interrupted their utterly absorbing sisterly gossip. And of course they made the most of the commercial breaks, as it were: they were the first to leave each lesson and the last to arrive at the next one.

The Challenge for the Comprehensive School by David Hargreaves

INDIVIDUALS

There are three letter Is in the word 'individual', four in 'individuality' – and classrooms contain 10, 20, 30 individuals. It's worth pausing to reflect on this fact. Overheard at parents' meeting: 'How does he cope with 30 of them?'

When children and young people in schools are asked, they invariably comment that their best teachers know them as individuals. In great classrooms, teachers know in depth their pupils' individual dispositions to learn, but never through the prism of a glass ceiling. Teachers recognise which teaching and learning styles are more effective and which are less effective. Above all, they have a clear grasp of the potential pupils have to develop their multiple intelligences, talents and aptitudes in various directions.

School and classrooms are inherently about academic and applied learning. They are also places unique in society where children come together to learn how to socialise. Social, moral, spiritual, cultural education is 'taught, caught and sought' through what happens in classrooms and the wider school community. During the pandemic period when most children were not at school, something significant was lost by way of social mixing for young people. What do pupils most miss when school is closed? Their mates.

Teachers serve 'in loco parentis', and how this manifests itself daily varies through the age ranges. If you ask parents what the most important thing for them is about schooling, they invariably say 'keeping my child safe'. (And how quickly parents tell a school if they feel their child's safety has been compromised.) Each child is unique and special, and a great classroom holds on to the fact that it is dealing with individuals first, groups of children second.

Gifted teachers in these classrooms try to see the learning opportunities and resources they present *through* the eyes of the individual pupil. They are ever on the lookout to identify the golden key in every child: her or his passions, dispositions, aptitudes, gifts. Ask any teacher, and successfully unlocking that key is so very satisfying professionally, especially if a pupil has been initially reluctant to open themselves up to the risk of failure.

Empathy is that vital capacity in a teacher to imagine and understand that the learner may well have a different frame of reference. The teacher tries to 'climb inside the learner's skin' to explain something in a different way so that the new idea or concept is grasped. Students value this greatly. To take some first-hand examples from classrooms:

- The Reception child who cannot manage to repeat a sound taught to her in a phonics lesson – until the teacher finds that sound in a song the child likes, and then she can repeat it, again and again and again.

- The Year 2 child who is having difficulty counting in evens and odds – until the teacher sits down with him and takes out some real coins to count – then he gets it, at once pocketing the money.

- The Year 4 child who is having difficulty telling the time – until the teacher takes a globe and a torch and explains the movement of the sun – then he grasps it, and smiles.

- The Year 6 child who cannot 'read between the lines' until the teacher finds a copy of Anthony Browne's *Zoo* and talks about the humans and the animals looking at each other through bars – then she can, and won't let go of the book.

- The Year 7 student who is struggling with present and past tenses in French – until the teacher shows some TV clips from 'les infos d'hier et d'aujourd'hui' – she comprehends.

- The Year 9 student who cannot handle the chisel correctly until the teacher spends time getting her to try subtly different handle grips, linked to her bike's handlebars, until at last one suits – she is delighted.

- The Year 11 student who is having difficulty with understanding irrational numbers – until the teacher shows him the golden ratio in art – he has an 'aha' moment.

- The Year 13 student who just cannot grasp redox reactions until seeing the colour changes of permanganate. The teacher talks through the practical experiment: the change from pink to green to brown solution. The student is happy she can now answer that exam question.

The daily reality in classrooms is that everyone is pressed for time. Yet in great classrooms the adult(s) somehow make(s) extra time to enable every child to progress at their optimum pace – seeking thoughtfully to extend them just that little extra pace. Most pupils most of the time will grasp even the most challenging of concepts, if given the chance to reflect, question, reflect again, and then practise.

The standard classroom doesn't fit everyone

Identifying a child's individual special need in timely fashion; addressing that need; reassessing at intervals; communicating carefully with everyone involved, especially parents – the process is as simple and potentially complex as that. Most schools today have well-thought-out provision for pupils who need in-classroom support, time out of the main classroom, time perhaps away from their peers for social reasons, time perhaps for intensive academic catch-up or keep-up.

In the best 'resource bases', variously titled, learning is intelligently bespoke and takes place in attractive rooms. These settings are led by well-trained, gifted practitioners able to balance strong interpersonal skills with robust expectations of what pupils 'off timetable' can achieve. They are highly reflective colleagues, ever questing to fine-tune their curriculum offer in response to students' predispositions to learning on a given day. To spend time in such zones for learning is to be in a great classroom.

Further, these teachers communicate effectively with parents about their children's progress and their plans to reintegrate them into the main timetable. How these pupils are supported and led to succeed is often a litmus test of the successful school. How a school treats its 'children on the margins' over time is a true test of its educational quality.

The standard school doesn't fit everybody

Experienced school leaders and teachers know that however accommodating, skilful and well meaning they are in curriculum design and pastoral support, mainstream school is not going to suit all comers. The homeschooling movement aside (still marginal pretty well anywhere in the world), alternative provision and pupil referral units are an important part of the educational estate in the UK.

In common with on-site resource bases, at their best, teachers and adults other than teachers (AOTs) are expertly trained to meet the sometimes very acute needs of youngsters who have experienced trauma of one kind or another, or who simply cannot fit readily into the everyday routines of their local primary or secondary school. In these contexts, with nuanced high expectations, the great classrooms are visually attractive, inviting to be in, and with purposeful activities at their heart. Staff are invariably able to have the patience and wisdom to move with agility between being the 'sage on the stage' and 'guide on the side', as students' learning needs determine.

A concluding image: on a visit with the headteacher to the large secondary school's alternative provision (ten minutes' walk), just as we were leaving a mother in the reception area said to the head: 'I can't thank you enough, Mr Hill. You have made our life at home happy again because of what you are doing for Davey here.' There is no better testament.

ASIDE

A poster in a bilingual school

La force d'une communauté se mesure au bien-être de ses membres les plus faibles.

The strength of a community is measured by the well-being of its weakest members.

Q. What posters and images in your classroom promote individual well-being?

JUDGEMENTS

This chapter is deliberately titled *Judgements* to assert the opening point that the teaching profession needs to develop an alternative vocabulary. Self-evidently the word has a judicial resonance, but in everyday, relaxed parlance we talk of 'you be the judge of that' or 'what's your judgement on that?' or 'that's good judgement'.

When it comes to schools and classrooms there is frequently an inspection vocabulary that haunts teachers, rooted in Ofsted's early days when inspectors, having 'judged' the lesson, gave a grade in a sealed envelope to a teacher. The days of sealed envelopes are long gone, but the poor/satisfactory/requires improvement/good/outstanding vocabulary lingers on – unhelpfully, and not in a spirit of appreciative enquiry.

The profession must put behind it the 'judgement' vocabulary and promote the language of *visitors* to lessons, not observers, and *reviewers* who work alongside and with teachers, not inspectors. Other countries do not have this cliff-edge approach to assessing teachers; there is no need for it. Great classrooms have their doors open to welcome any visitor to call by and appreciate the teaching and learning double act: colleagues and visitors are there to share ideas and fine-tune practice, not to judge and improve.

****

Great classrooms are characterised by highly reflective teachers: self-reflecting and reflecting with their pupils on how teaching and learning could be even richer and smarter in everyone's interests.

The first stage of self-reflection must include self-preservation: living and thriving to teach another day. Often attributed to Hippocrates, the man considered to be the father of medicine, is the phrase 'Physician, Heal Thyself'. To teachers and school leaders I say in like spirit: 'Pace Yourself.' Teaching is a relentless business, tiring and demanding no matter how fit you are or how positive you feel each morning about your work, your vocation, your purpose.

As a young teacher I was twice sent home from school by the legendary Miss Wallace. She had been an indefatigable senior nurse in London's Blitz (1940–1941) and, when I encountered her in a south London comprehensive, she was a warmly ferocious deputy head. She scanned the staffroom each morning to see that we were all fit to teach. On one occasion she looked at me closely and diagnosed conjunctivitis, and on another informed me that I had nits. She instructed me to go home. I didn't. In a large school I was able to steal away and teach, such was my determination never to have a day off. She forgave my youthful stubbornness.

Great classrooms are led by such teachers. They are equally self-critical about their own teaching techniques, always questing to revise resources and approaches to topics which will better enable students' understanding. They find peer review is invaluable and supportive in this context.

Next comes reflecting *with* students. In great classrooms time is set aside at intervals for teachers and pupils to reflect together on the learning journey, on what students are finding accessible and fun, upon what they are finding more challenging and less enjoyable.

This can be done formally through online questionnaires (see the Aside at the end of this chapter), through in-class quizzes and through individual, group and whole-class discussions. Colleagues in teams sometimes swap classes to carry this out in a slightly different, 'more objective', way, and always report how enjoyable it is to talk to another class covering the same curriculum that they are teaching. It matters not how such feedback is gathered, but it is a vital part of the commerce and reflection of great classrooms.

****

In the Inner London Education Authority (ILEA) of the early 1980s – with its abundance of subject resources created by teachers, curriculum and examination innovation, and rich opportunities for professional development – emerged an excellent pamphlet called 'Keeping the School Under Review'. It was a pioneering publication to encourage the newly emerging theme in the UK (its origins in the US) of self-evaluation, at whole-school and classroom level.

Subsequent decades have seen an industrialisation of institutional, department and phase self-evaluation to the point where the profession is most accomplished at it. One is minded to say that the majority of schools and colleges are so proficient that it renders external inspection (introduced in England in 1992) largely redundant – an argument for another day.

In great classrooms, teachers are avid consumers of different ways of keeping their practice under review. The Teachers' Standards (see pages 201–204) play a central role in most schools' systems for appraisal and performance management, however configured, and Early Careers Teachers benchmark their progress against the eight standards.

Teachers new to the profession are inevitably influenced by the practices of their colleagues, and in shaping their own style in the classroom learn generously from their peers what will work for them and what won't. We all have vivid memories of watching colleagues make mistakes and avowing that we'll not make those same ones, equally aware that we'll make our own mistakes, which in turn others will learn from.

How do great classrooms keep themselves effectively under review? The answer is that successful schools adopt different systems and pro-formas to suit their context, shaped very much by their views on 'accountability'. They ask themselves *why* and *for what purpose* are we designing a process – and design accordingly.

With a renewed focus on pupils' well-being and mindset, one useful self-evaluation framework encourages teachers and peer reviewers to ask whether students are:

- active participants in activities, stretching themselves in what they do and think, taking risks in their learning
- motivated, positively reinforced by their own achievements, reward systems and feedback

- enthusiastic about their learning, showing curiosity and taking the opportunity to lead and extend their own learning
- engaging with supportive relationships, collaborating, and benefiting from positive student–adult dialogue
- demonstrating self-discipline, regulating their own thoughts, managing their time and attention
- showing tolerance and sensitivity to those around them, co-operating, sharing and communicating in supportive ways
- persevering to achieve their best
- employing optimism and a growth mindset, seeking solutions and accepting mistakes as a condition of success.

As with all such checklists, the words and phrases essentially focus on the climate for learning, on the interaction between everyone in the classroom. If you are sitting in a special, primary or secondary classroom where most of the above are present most of the time, you are arguably sitting in a great classroom.

In another context, an all-through school decided to eschew the redundant vocabulary of inspection referred to in the opening paragraphs above, and has devised its own Pedagogical Framework, reflecting a range of international research (see pages 183–189). At its core is the language of a teacher assessing themselves as 'confident' or 'instructor'; the descriptors are used in self- and peer-review, calibrated by line managers.

For example, in relation to one of the seven aspects of excellent practice 'Reviewing Material', the teacher can self-evaluate against the following descriptors:

Confident

'The teacher begins most lessons with a short review of previous learning. Clear links are made between new and previous learning. Students are given opportunities to overlearn new skills, knowledge and concepts.'

Instructor

'The teacher is especially adept at identifying the skills, knowledge and concepts and instilling the attitude that students will need to master.

Careful planning of the consolidation of new skills and concepts is evident in all lessons.'

The words are important, yes. Equally vital in great classrooms is what the words do to help teachers reflect deeply on their practice. To my mind, this framework marks a potential breakthrough in how teachers in great classrooms can self-evaluate in a new language which firmly leaves behind the tired language of formal inspection. This school's complementary professional development portfolios complete the picture.

****

It is in our nature as teachers to look around us and wonder at and about other teachers. For me, there was Helena, who was a concentration camp survivor with her number stamped on her arm, taught art with her sleeves rolled up, and commanded instant silence; there was Jane, a petite teacher of French who had a soft voice and the 'cold eye' that held all ages in her linguistic spells; there was Richard, whose personal warmth and skills with young children were palpable, inimitable; there was Clifford, my first mentor, whose breadth of subject knowledge was humbling.

They were in their different ways children at heart, fearless of failure, risk-takers, improvisers, mavericks in the true sense of the word. I admired them. I could never seek to emulate their ways of doing. We must each carve out our own.

ASIDE

Rate your teacher

This example was in the form of a QR code on the doors of classrooms in an international school, devised by teachers in a faculty to get prompt feedback from their students. Teachers and students alike enjoyed this dialogue planned at sensible intervals.

Use a scale of 1 (highest) to 4 (lowest)

1. The classroom is an environment where I feel encouraged, can voice my opinion and can be valued as an individual.

2. My teacher sets clear expectations for my behaviour.

3. My teacher sets clear expectations for my studies and the quality of my work, and reinforces these verbally and by showing me what is expected.

4. Learning experiences in the classes are varied and challenging.

5. My teacher caters for my learning style and my ability level.

6. My teacher provides me with suitable resources and reading material.

7. When I have difficulties, I am encouraged and motivated to improve my performance.

8. My teacher returns assessed work promptly.

9. My teacher provides me with useful comments on my assessed work.

10. I understand the assessment criteria that my teacher is using.

Q. What do you think of this questionnaire? How do you gain useful feedback from your pupils?

KUDOS

'kudos' *noun*

– praise given for achievement
– fame and renown from an act or achievement

How do we recognise the work of those teachers who create great classrooms?

Importantly for the profession, how do we make sure we retain good colleagues, recruit the brightest and best in a market of competing professions, *and* ensure that over time more and more teachers develop into top practitioners? Public recognition through local, regional and national awards is more commonplace today than even a decade ago. What has long been true is that school leaders have always made a point of nurturing and praising teachers' best practices. And teachers enjoy being appreciated by their peers!

Teachers rarely enter the profession to gain fame and renown, though in our 24/7 news and social media culture, increasing numbers of teachers across the world have become well known, providing online materials and ideas for classrooms. In-service education, once a local Cinderella service, is now an international business, with teachers securing their professional development across continents.

And through a wide range of regional and national hubs in the UK, an exciting generation of teachers-as-trainers and teachers-as-authors has emerged. Their influence is being felt, and contributes to the profession feeling good about itself and demonstrating the impact well-informed teachers are having on children and young people in schools.

Professional communities, virtual and in-person, enable mutual trust, praise and recognition, and raise the profile of teaching in society.

One of the long-standing paradoxes in any profession is that the highly competent and confident practitioners often get promoted away from the very workplace that drew them into the profession. It is as true in medicine and law as it is in accountancy and teaching (architects are an interesting exception). If you're not careful, those who are gifted teachers are drawn away to manage and lead others, their gifts thus lost to students in classrooms. It may not be as stark as this in the right quarters, but promotion and remuneration structures are not always conducive to ensuring that the best teachers keep teaching.

Advanced Skills Teachers was one model introduced into the system to keep excellent teachers in the classroom, and had its merits especially with outreach across partnerships of special, primary and secondary schools. When the current Teachers' Standards were introduced in 2011, a supplementary set of Master Standards was also drafted, though not formally adopted at the time by the DfE. Within these lie a set of descriptors which many schools and multi-academy trusts across the country now use as a way of appraising, recognising and rewarding practitioners in great classrooms. There are five key aspects, extracts as follows:

A. *Knowledge*

   Master Teachers have deep and extensive knowledge of their specialism, going far beyond the set programmes they teach. They have an intrinsic curiosity about their specialism, keep up with developments, and their teaching reflects their own passion and expertise. They respond intelligently and confidently to the unexpected and wide-ranging questions their pupils are encouraged to ask, and they are able to lead discussions and explorations which take pupils beyond the confines of teaching programmes.

B. *Classroom Performance*

   Master Teachers command the classroom, skilfully leading, encouraging and extending pupils. They have the respect of both pupils and parents. They are at ease in their role, and discipline and dialogue are unselfconscious and effective. Teaching is motivating, often inspiring, and basic principles are expertly taught. Expectations are challengingly high, realistic, based on sound experience, and take into account the abilities of all pupils.

C. *Outcomes*

The Master Teacher's meticulous planning and organisation ensure that pupils are well prepared for all forms of assessment. Outcomes achieved by pupils in the context in question are outstanding. They have an awareness of school, national and international benchmarks and examination reports, including data from maintained and independent schools.

D. *Environment and Ethos*

The class is one in which pupils feel welcome and valued. There is a stimulating culture of scholarship alongside a sense of mutual respect and good manners. The Master Teacher has an excellent rapport with classes and individual pupils. The classroom environment created to support study and activities is an inspirational example of practice, appropriate to the age range or phase.

E. *Professional Context*

Master Teachers are highly regarded by colleagues, who want to learn from them. They willingly play a role in the development of school policies and in the professional life of the school. They work in collaboration with colleagues on pastoral and wider pupil-related matters, giving advice as appropriate. They engage with and contribute to professional networks beyond the school.

Master Teachers are open in the giving and receiving of professional advice, which may include coaching or mentoring colleagues and less experienced teachers. They work to significant effect with other adults in ensuring high quality education for the pupils they serve.

Each of the above is worth careful study and reflection on in relation to what happens in great classrooms. They offer some universal truths. A comparative reading of what other countries set down as the key constituents of excellent classrooms reveals a not dissimilar set of characteristics.

The final paragraph of Professional Context above is worth especial note. In the daily commerce of any school community there tend to be 'go-to' people, highly respected by their colleagues and always seeming to have time to give to others. This paragraph is describing such colleagues, by definition acknowledging their contribution to school life. Praise and kudos may not be explicitly expressed but are implicitly present.

A wise headteacher once observed that the challenge in keeping high standards in any school – and society's expectations are always rising – lay not so much in the proverbial 'teaching old dogs new tricks' but rather in 'getting old dogs to *unlearn* old tricks'. He was expressing the view that whilst new teachers were generally quick to pick up on fresh initiatives, longer-standing teachers were sometimes reluctant to change ways of doing. This is human nature: change can feel threatening.

Great classrooms are led by Master Teachers who have mastered their craft yet are ever questing to improve and develop their practice, and who openly and generously share that journey with colleagues. The classrooms are led by those who, whatever their chronological age, are 'young at heart', able to adapt their practices to the spirit of the times.

ASIDE

President Pranab Mukherjee of India. 2016 Teachers' Day

'Teachers' Day is an occasion when we recognise the dedicated services of the teachers of our nation, who are engaged in building and strengthening the intellectual and ethical foundations of our children.

'A sound education system is the bedrock of an enlightened society. Inspired teachers are the building blocks of a good education system.

'An inspired teacher links the individual goals of the students to the societal and national goals. We need our teachers to instil in our children civilisational values of sacrifice, tolerance, pluralism, understanding and compassion. Out teachers also need to imbibe technology and new methodologies to create modern and effective approaches to teaching and learning.

'I convey my good wishes to the entire teaching community of our country and express gratitude on behalf of the people of our nation for their lifetime of dedication and commitment to the great cause of educating our youth.'

Q. What would you include in a speech on a Teachers' Day which had the effect of praising teachers?

LEARN

Why do we learn what we learn?

The 19th century author and Her Majesty's Inspector Matthew Arnold memorably observed that a good modern society can only come about when all its citizens are educated in 'the best that has been thought and said'. Different cultures interpret 'the best' variously, but that assertion probably leads to the subject-based curriculum, for better or worse, with which we are all familiar.

Any national curriculum, anywhere in the world, is passing on to the next generation the nation's history, traditions and values. Equally, that curriculum is preparing students for today's and tomorrow's global society with skills and knowledge the nation believes will be of value. In the UK over many years there has been a political debate about which shall come first: skills *or* curriculum, curriculum *or* skills? This futile discussion falls into 'the tyranny of either/or'. No! It is 'and/and'.

In Ian McEwan's novel *The Children Act* (which everyone working with children should read), he writes of a judge having to make a momentous decision as to whether or not to turn off the life-support machine of a 17-year-old boy. In coming to her decision, the judge is described as follows:

> She listed some relevant ingredients, goals towards which a child might grow.
>
> Economic and moral freedom, virtue, compassion and altruism, satisfying work through engagement with demanding tasks, a flourishing network of personal relationships, earning the esteem of others, pursuing larger meanings to one's existence,

and having at the centre of one's life one or a small number of significant relations defined above all by love.

School prospectuses across the land set out their aims for pupils, but rarely will you come across a more succinct description of 'goals towards which a child might grow'. What characterises the best schools and the great classrooms of the world is that they have thought through what it is the pupil needs to learn to be a thriving global citizen, beyond what a specific national curriculum might dictate.

Imagine for a moment meeting someone you teach now – could be 7 or 15 years of age – when they are 27, and you meet them in a Miami beach bar. What kind of person do you want to meet? When I ask this question of teachers anywhere in the world, they speak of wanting to meet someone who is happy, healthy, confident, 'at ease in their skin', content with their lives. Rarely does anyone say 'a student with a top degree'. One teacher said: 'they buy me a drink'!

Thus it is worth asking ourselves whether what we teach at school and how we organise learning are sufficiently focused on the individual person, their character, their social health, and their unique brain and aptitudes.

Great classrooms from ages 3 to 19, in my judgement, have identified what Howard Gardner terms 'five minds for the future'. (Significantly, Gardner's early research work focused on multiple intelligences.) He argues that the 21st century belongs to people who think in certain ways:

the disciplined mind, schooled in basic subjects such as history, science and art but, crucially, a master of one profession, vocation or craft

the synthesising mind, which can make sense of disparate pieces of information

the creating mind, capable of asking new questions and finding imaginative answers.

the respectful mind, which shows an appreciation of different cultures.

the ethical mind, which enables one to behave responsibly as a worker and citizen.

Designing and delivering a whole-school curriculum that challenges these five minds is the hallmark of the vibrant, dynamic classroom of today and tomorrow. Teachers in these classrooms think creatively about what content is being taught, and how each student with his or her different learning style is being accommodated. This is no easy task, but clarity about what we learn and why is essential to underpin daily planning and desired outcomes – always remembering that unintended outcomes are sometimes just as important.

Engaging parents in this enterprise through discussion, publications or on the school website is worthwhile, so that they too see that learning at school is not just about subject matter and skills acquisition – it is about something much bigger: something that prepares their children to be thriving young citizens.

A number of schools have developed an exciting competencies-led curriculum fit for the 21st century learner, again reflecting a clarity of vision about the broad purposes of schooling. Ecolint in Geneva is one such school that seeks to focus on the process of learning in the broadest sense: intellectual, creative, social, ethical and physical development. Its seven core competencies are:

- lifelong learning
- self-agency
- interactively using diverse tools and resources
- interacting with others
- interacting with the world
- multi-literateness
- trans-disciplinary.

(See pages 198–199 for further details.)

And another comparator, which creates highly motivating classrooms, is the work of Deborah Eyre: 'High Performance Learning', and is centred on schools having Seven Pillars:

1. Mindset shift
2. Enquiry-based learning

3. Expertise development
4. Practice and training
5. Feedback
6. Engagement of parents
7. 'With' students not 'to' them.

(https://www.highperformancelearning.co.uk/)

****

What teachers, by definition, are generally very good at is possessing a body of knowledge which they seek to communicate to their pupils. What one might term 'academic learning' is a real strength in schools; and so it should be given the investments most nations make in educating their teachers to degree level and beyond.

In the great classroom it is often 'applied learning' that moves the lesson to a higher level. Watch a group of 6-year-olds introduced to planting their own watercress or a group of 15-year-olds dissecting a kidney for the first time. The teacher has rehearsed the theory with them, but the application of knowledge and skills is where real learning is embedded and begins to flourish.

It may be stating the obvious, but to observe, in a further education college, a skilled bricklayer tutor sharing his skills and passion with students, and watching them gradually master techniques at a basic level, is to witness great learning.

I contest that 'difficulty is pleasurable': challenge in classrooms should be made pleasurable or students will tumble at the first obstacle. When I assert to audiences of teachers that we need to make pupils 'cry intellectually' once a week, they frequently look askance. If I say 'wobble intellectually' they are happier, though that risks softening my argument. The reality is that for most of us acquiring a new skill it is a heady mix of perspiration, repetition, frustration, humour and memorable light-bulb moments.

Even in great classrooms there will be moments of tedium and 'this work is too easy Miss', but there is no escaping that to go the extra intellectual mile, the best teachers seize every opportunity to move a mathematical or linguistic or design concept to a point where pupils are left wondering, even momentarily lost. And this links to praise in classrooms being well earned, and not handed out emptily so that its intention is undermined. Great teachers judge all this so well.

Which brings us to what various researchers and commentators refer to as *deep learning*. To achieve this, all the ingredients of great classrooms need to come together. First, outcomes and success criteria are set with sophistication and challenge. Second, lesson planning harnesses enquiry questions, rich texts and building-learning-power techniques: experiential and cognitive elements combine. Third, collaboration gives students a safe learning environment in which to take risks and perform with confidence. (And see the Aside below.)

****

To conclude where this chapter began: Why do we learn what we learn? International educator Conrad Hughes sees schooling in the 2020s in this way:

> International education is at a turning point. We are moving from international-mindedness to inter-cultural sensitivity. From factual regurgitation to deep conceptual understanding. From skills to competences. And from narrow high-stakes assessments to a more inclusive and generous celebration of learning.

> Let's see the gifts in every child. Let's make those gifts radiate, powerful stars that shine light on the world. Let's do this.

ASIDE

Deep learning

- Quality of independent work, and students helping each other out, is noticeable when the teacher is not in the room or working with individuals.
- Range and sophistication of planned questioning techniques lead to deep thinking.

- Specific, regular 'challenge marking' and feedback provide a dialogue which allows pupils to learn from mistakes and make rapid progress.
- Critiquing protocols lead to multiple drafts and beautiful work.
- Group work allows students to take on varied roles, wear several 'hats', and learn how to work as a team, in pursuit of quality outcomes.
- Lessons are differentiated by clever use of data, skilful working with additional adults, and tailored resources so that each child pursues personal challenges as well as lesson objectives.
- Quality talk in pairs, trios, individually and in larger groups is scaffolded, modelled and deployed to enhance thinking and learning.
- Pupils acquire and practise skills and dispositions, as well as knowledge, and end the lesson as better learners.
- Newest technologies are used to accelerate progress and give students access to the best possible learning tools and resources.

Q. Which aspects of classroom practice listed here contribute effectively to younger and older pupils' deep learning?

READING 4

I don't know what it was that interested me so much. Part of it might have been that she talked so fast. She talked a blue streak, at about a hundred miles an hour, and that made it feel as if it wasn't just another boring lesson. Most of the teachers I've had talk horribly slowly. Some of them actually come out with the words at half speed, and others sound as if they're talking normally at first, but when you pay attention you realise that they're repeating themselves over and over again, first for the thicks in the back row, and then for all the people who've only just come in because they've been mucking about in the changing rooms, and then, one last time, for all those who've been there the whole time but simply weren't bothering to listen.

The Book of the Banshee by Anne Fine

MARKING

...AND FEEDBACK...

At secondary school I had the great good fortune to be taught English by Oliver Goldfinch. Most of us can think of one inspirational, stand-out teacher whom we remember vividly from our own schooldays. OG was that man for me. Amongst his many talents and idiosyncrasies was his marking of English essays. His calligraphy was an art in its own right; his comments were eulogies and scoldings in equal measure, always with a hint of humour and 'let's not take things too seriously even though the exam is around the corner'.

Strikingly, for all comments that were positive he used his *red* fountain pen; for all critical comments he used his *black* fountain pen. Marking in this way must have taken him many, many hours; the good results of his students were there for all to see. His verbal feedback in class was just as colourful and robust.

Feedback is the fuel that propels the acquisition of knowledge and the embedding of newly acquired skills. Interviewed anywhere in the world, children and young people speak consistently about how much they value the teacher who:

- marks and signs their work regularly (children love their teacher's signature)
- praises and critiques as appropriate, orally and in writing
- indicates how next-best-steps to improve can be made
- draws careful attention to examination and test requirements.

At the heart of great classrooms is that teacher determination to appraise and value what students are producing, indicating strengths and 'even-better-ifs', and, where examinations demand, grading work against agreed frameworks. One primary school captures its practice concisely as follows, a fair manifesto in any setting:

Marking and feedback should:

- respond to individual learning needs, via oral feedback and written comments from the teacher
- be accessible to children and manageable for teachers
- relate to the learning intention and success criteria
- comment on previous attainment within the curricular target
- give recognition and praise for achievement
- give clear strategies for improvement
- allow specific time for children to read, reflect and respond to marking
- inform future planning and target setting
- use consistent codes across the school
- be seen by children as a positive approach to improve their learning.

Assessment and evaluation of pupils by their teachers comes in many forms and is a widely researched topic internationally, whether applied to the early years or to higher education. Different contexts variously interpret and harness formative, summative, peer and self-assessment – appropriate to age range and subject matter.

In essence, teachers are focused on what progress pupils are making towards intended goals, whether learning to count to 100 or produce an A grade politics essay. Skilled marking is charting and commenting upon that progress and, at its best, spotting potential so that students are enabled to achieve beyond what they originally thought possible. Feedback at its best *is* high-octane learning fuel.

In the first years of schooling, oral feedback plays a significant part in the learning journey, in-the-moment verbal interventions from staff wishing to steer a child in a particular direction, or improve their basic skills, or help them socialise with their peers. Verbal feedback remains the most dynamic form of assessment in every nursery and Reception classroom; as pupils move up through their primary years this is complemented by the kind of written feedback listed in the manifesto above. (The use of the SeeSaw portfolio for sharing young children's daily achievements with parents is highly valued.)

In great primary classrooms, teachers make time to go through and mark work with children on an individual basis, for each of us makes our own pattern of errors on any journey of learning. Those teachers make children feel that they have 'failed wisely' or 'succeeded superbly' in order to bolster self-esteem and promote the next phase of learning.

Formal peer assessment emerges as a feature in the upper primary years; and in the best classrooms it is thoughtfully prepared for and modelled meaningfully by teachers. That same peer assessment grows in importance through the secondary years, and in great classrooms it has a decisive impact on pupils' progress.

What is self-evidently the case in secondary schools is that as students move to different subject areas *how* they are assessed varies and therefore how teachers mark and intervene in pupils' progress varies too. The marking of history or English essays is one type of written feedback, and in the best classrooms it is done with meticulous attention to constructive detail; the live verbal feedback by the design or art teacher is pivotal in shaping a drawing or a product, and so too in music or physical education where teachers comment on technique; in science or maths, students value a prompt and an explanation to help them complete a tricky problem or experiment. Shared 'final' performance or generously evaluating a pupil's 'beautiful work' is equally valued by all.

In great classrooms, whatever kind of feedback is being deployed, it is the dialogue between teacher and pupils, and between pupils themselves, that is the oil of understanding. These deliberate and unintended interactions further pupils' thinking, embed self-assessment, and allow students to think positively about what they have achieved and where they are going next in a particular subject.

A note on grades

In 1913 the American education researcher I.E. Finkelstein wrote as follows:

> When we consider the practically universal use in all educational institutions of a system of marks, whether numbers or letters, to indicate scholastic attainment of the pupils, and when we remember how very great stress is laid by teachers and pupils alike upon these marks as real measures or indicators of attainment, we can but be astonished at the blind faith that has been felt in the reliability of the marking system.

Everything has been thought of before; the challenge is to think of it again. Debate will ever be present on the subject of the reliability of grades and grading systems. We live in an imperfect world and seek to improve things. In great classrooms, teachers do profitably share with students that debate. They emphasise too that yes, the grade is important, but so too are the comments I have made on your work. The practice of hiding the grade until the student has read the comments is well tested.

****

I once heard a head of department say – as colleagues were groaning under the weight of Year 13 mock exam marking – 'every job has its equivalent of Sunday night marking'. An animated conversation ensued about colleagues' experiences of other jobs and careers and what that Sunday night equivalent was.

Suffice to say, the marking of books and essays features high in any list teachers give of the most time-consuming aspect of their profession. It is both an undoubted slog *and* essential. The slog naturally brings job satisfaction in the form of teachers realising how well they have taught something as seen through the high quality of students' responses.

My own personal way of dealing with the Sunday slog over 20 years was, very energetically on a Monday, to carry a set of well-marked exercise books into my Year 9 class and assert: 'I spent four hours last night marking these books. I'm now resting. I am giving you 20 minutes to do justice to my marking. Go!' This remains a favourite theme of mine when reviewing schools: in great classrooms pupils work harder than their teachers and are certainly *doing justice* to the teachers' marking. Pupils owe that to their teachers, every time.

The marking of tests and examination papers has existed as long as teaching, and Oliver Goldfinch, with whom this chapter opened, was a master marker in a long line of great teachers that stretches to this day. Movements such as 'No More Marking', rooted in solid research, provide innovative alternatives; and emerging AI technology – with all its controversies – perhaps promises a much-needed lightening of teacher workload in assessment. The profession prays that it just might.

ASIDE

The McNamara fallacy

The first step is to measure whatever can be easily measured. This is OK as far as it goes.

The second step is to disregard that which can't be easily measured or to give it an arbitrary quantitative value. This is artificial and misleading.

The third step is to presume that what can't be measured easily really isn't important. This is blindness.

The fourth step is to say what can't be easily measured really doesn't exist. This is suicide.

Q. Where in assessment of students do we risk falling into any of the traps above?

NEOLOGISMS

'neologism' *noun*

– the coining or use of new words

> Developments in neuroscience now lie at the heart of teacher training courses, where aspirant teachers are being taught in a more rigorous and evidence-based manner than ever before. To become a teacher in the 21st century means to understand how memory works and how we remember, it means to have an awareness of the best cognitive conditions for learning, and, crucially, it means to keep up to date with the latest research so as not to be left behind. (Harry Hudson)

It was not always this way. As recently as 20 years ago, the terms initial training, induction and in-service training shaped the landscape and in a way, frankly, which did not match the demands expected in other leading professions.

The advent of the phrase 'continuous professional development' to describe what goes on in schools today is a relatively recent phenomenon, and it is still not linked as in other professions to teachers fulfilling a certain number of hours per annum in order to keep a licence to practise. Arguably, until teaching makes this a requirement, it will not join other professions at the top table.

Great classrooms have always been led by teachers who take their own professional development seriously, and if they happened to work in the right schools where leaders valued that development they thrived. Even a decade ago, not enough schools took that professional development as being a cornerstone of a flourishing education community.

With the advent in 2011 of the Education Endowment Foundation (EEF) and the subsequent birth of Research Schools, the explosion in new technologies, alongside a new generation of teachers passionate about evidence-based research informing their practice – in many ways continuous professional development has come of age. The impact in classrooms is there to see. Experienced colleagues talk about 'the shock of the new' as a fresh vocabulary about the science – not just the art – of teaching is in the air.

(It is worth a passing comment here that the EEF has been particularly helpful to teachers in improving reading standards and addressing disadvantage, both still work in progress across all schools. And the organisation has done much to mitigate political interference with classroom practices.)

Reflect for a moment on the way some of the following vocabulary is now quite commonplace in staffrooms, courses, training sessions, EduTwitter, TeacherMeet and the like:

NEUROSCIENCE

INTRINSIC, EXTRANEOUS, GERMANE LOAD

COGNITIVE PSYCHOLOGY   **PRINCIPLES OF INSTRUCTION**

COGNITIVE OVERLOAD   RETRIEVAL   MULTI-MODAL MEANING

CURRICULUM SEQUENCING   META-COGNITION   SELF-REGULATION

KNOWLEDGE ORGANISERS   RECURSIVE FEEDBACK

PURPOSEFUL ORACY   ADAPTIVE STRATEGIES

MODELLING AND SCAFFOLDING

GROWTH MINDSET

The list of neologisms continues. Whilst these are not words new to the dictionary, their usage in the teaching profession *is* new, and it is fascinating to talk to teachers in great classrooms about how they are harnessing recent and current research to inform their practice. Teachers are familiar with the images of 'sage on the stage' and 'guide on the side' – now we are moving towards the teacher as 'learning scientist'.

Some would argue that the best teachers have long been implicitly aware of meta-cognition, self-regulation and growth mindset – and that these neologisms are fancy terms for what they have always practised. That may be the case, but 21st century great classrooms are undoubtedly the richer for teachers being able to converse in a language about high quality learning that is research-based. Further, what some commentators describe as the 'democratisation' of teaching, with teachers playing an increased role in the direction of pedagogy, means teachers have greater agency in their own practice.

I recently tuned into a conversation amongst a talented group of Year 6 teachers planning a biology (they didn't call it 'science') topic. One referred to 'intrinsic cognitive load' when talking about the innate and appropriate difficulty of the task they were planning for the children. Another built on that to explain 'extraneous cognitive load' as over-busy learning and cluttered resources often distracting some students. A third talked of the ideal of the 'germane cognitive load' where the children can link new concepts with their long-term memory to make the required breakthrough in understanding. I was fascinated.

William Gibson, author of the 1984 influential novel *Necromancer,* observed cannily that the future is already here, but it's just not very evenly distributed. In many forward-thinking schools, research-based evidence has played its part for decades. Teachers naturally build on their predecessors' knowledge, intuition and skills. Many curriculum schemes and examination syllabuses have for years been rooted in school- and university-based development work: think of Nuffield mathematics, Salters' Chemistry, the International Baccalaureate.

It is in the past decade in particular where schools around the world have been adopting more common approaches (some would use the term 'brands') to classroom practices, with origins in research and tried and tested practice. *Teach like a Champion* by Doug Lemov, and Barak Rosenshine's *Principles of Instruction*, the latter first conceived more than three decades ago, are two such favoured by many teachers.

A leading Chief Education Officer once observed about a short, very well-crafted handbook he had written to guide his local education authority staff that it became 'a vision that blinded', by which he meant colleagues stuck too closely to its script, and cramped individual initiative. Whilst there is always a danger of the development of orthodoxies, empty buzzwords and meaningless neologisms, current consensus thinking about effective teaching revolves around the following, variously worded in different settings:

- Care about helping your kids to do the best that they can.
- Understand but don't excuse your students.
- Be clear about what you want your students to learn.
- Disseminate surface knowledge and promote deep learning.
- Gradually release responsibility for learning.
- Give your students feedback.
- Involve students in learning from each other.
- Manage your students' behaviour.
- Evaluate the impact you are having on your students.
- Continue learning ways that you can be of even more help to more students.

As a recipe for a successful classroom, it's a fine one, rooted in what great teachers have done for generations and making explicit what most teachers do implicitly. As a starting point for a trainee teacher, it has considerable merit.

What is equally important to put alongside this 'what the teacher does' is 'what students find that works'. Talking to students across age ranges and contexts, they say, in colloquial terms, that the teacher should do the following three simple things to help their learning:

- Chunk it up.
- Sum it up.

- Give us time to think.

Teaching and learning is a special double act. Great classrooms today are undoubtedly enhanced by the neologisms which, over time, will no longer be new but common parlance in staffrooms. It is highly likely that AI technologies – thus far largely unrealised in schools but arriving at a desk near you soon – will bring the next generation of new vocabulary to the profession.

ASIDE

A new profession called teaching

(Source: *Must Do Better* by Hudson & Blatchford)

- To be a teacher would be considered in the same breath as being an accountant, pilot, lawyer, architect or doctor. Teaching isn't for other people's children. It's for your own children.
- The teacher in society is viewed as an academic expert, a guru, a source of knowledge. Teachers have a recognised and valued role in society to educate current and future generations of confident and adaptable citizens well prepared for the challenges of the 21st century.
- The teacher is paid well, benchmarked internationally – a reflection of their value in society.
- Teachers are deemed an essential public service, talked of with the same reverence as judges and medics, and teaching has a universally recognised national brand.
- Teachers have a contract that commits them to a certain number of days of teaching, as well as a set number of days of certificated professional development in order to keep their licence to teach.
- Teachers have paid sabbaticals and flexible conditions of service to enable them to teach to 75.

- Entry requirements for teaching are set at a minimum of a 2.1 degree for new entrants. Those joining at a later stage must have equivalent qualifications.

Q. What are your views on this list? What would you like to see added over the coming thirty years in projecting the future role of the teacher?

OUTDOORS

It is natural to think 'indoors' when thinking about classrooms, certainly in the UK. Google the word 'classroom' as it relates to different cultures and countries, and other locations for learning appear colourfully and in a way that challenges assumptions of where successful learning can take place.

Elsewhere in this book, the argument has been made that great classrooms routinely 'shift' 10 per cent of learning out of the classroom window so that students apply what they are learning to the real world and make connections across disciplines.

Let's think imaginatively about what we mean by 'outdoors' in relation to schooling. This chapter offers a number of snapshots for stepping outside...

- *Indoors/outdoors*

  I recall visiting a junior school in Lake Country, north of Toronto. Hidden deep in woodlands the school had an amazing outdoor curriculum, whatever the weather: no such thing as bad weather, just the wrong clothing. With open plan in building design and campus layout, at break-times the children had to follow just one rule. They could roam far and wide into the woods and fields (bears live there) as long as at any one time they could see the top of the school's flagpole, a singular point for orientation. The children loved that freedom to roam – and be children.

  In another context, Grove Primary in inner-city Birmingham – in response to the cramped housing conditions and limited play facilities which many of the 700+ children occupy – turned its curriculum for three- to seven-year-olds into an outdoor experience for half the week. With precious little outdoor space surrounding the school and all of it hard surfaces, school leaders were wonderfully imaginative in creating beaches, copses, topic dens and soft play areas in which outdoor musical instruments, waterfalls and large mathematical shapes provide memorable stimuli for children. It can be done.

In both of the above examples, the outdoor and the indoor curriculum were skilfully woven together, as they frequently are in great early years classrooms. It is a distinctive feature of so many primary schools today, urban and rural, that leaders and teachers have invested in inventive and creative outdoor learning environments, and planned aspects of the curriculum around different zones in playgrounds, fields and woods.

And how the Forest School concept has been brilliantly developed and variously interpreted across this country to provide great 'classroom' experiences and curriculum provision for children and young people. To watch an expert leading learning in this arena – across primary, special and secondary – is to witness how motivated pupils can be by being in fresh air with active, purposeful play and study their shared focus. Learning is owned by pupils and is by its very nature intriguingly organic and open-ended. The 'teaching torch' quickly passes to pairs and groups of children exploring and 'owning' a natural environment.

- *Visitors in/visits out*

  A relatively easy aspect of extending the curriculum to bring the outdoors inside is by inviting visitors into classrooms, from fire engines appearing outside nursery and Reception classrooms to poets, cartographers, politicians, 'mathemagicians', local farmers and shopkeepers enlivening assemblies and classrooms for all ages. Protocols around hosting visitors and guests in school are vital for all involved. What visitors bring is their personal and professional experiences, which can be eye-opening for students and, in some cases, truly inspirational and life-changing for individual pupils who suddenly become motivated to apply themselves to their studies focused on a new ambition.

This same building of pupils' cultural capital, broadening horizons and exposure to wider society, characterises visits out of school: to art galleries and museums, concerts and theatres, ancient ruins and battlefields. In going on day trips locally – to the capital city, to the coast or the country – the student experience is enriched, very often linked to a curriculum topic. Indeed, displays in special and primary classrooms in particular are frequently a vivid reminder of a day visit to a river, castle or shoreline, or a school journey into an unfamiliar environment.

GCSE and A level fieldwork and visits range widely across different subjects; in great classrooms what is noticeable is how effectively the teacher has harnessed such a visit to bring a topic vividly alive and will refer to it routinely to help students remember new vocabulary, theories, diagrams, concepts and ideas. Work experience for senior students brings similarly fresh perspectives, including the important recognition that work is not all play; and many students comment that the greatest value of work experience has been realising the kind of employment they *don't* want to pursue.

- *Voices aloud*

Ask any adult what they most remember about school. It may well be visits to the theatre or school journeys mentioned above. They are certain to include times when they were not with their usual class friends but working across age groups in orchestras, plays and other groupings organised by the school.

Aside from the small primary containing mixed-age classes, opportunities to learn along with children from different age groups are too infrequent in schools. Leaders and teachers recognise this, and in successful schools opportunities are maximised through after-school clubs of all descriptions. The creative arts are often the most popular: music, dance, drama and 'performance' in its widest sense – performance that gives the chance for youngsters who enjoy and are skilled at using their bodies and voices to entertain others.

Every teacher knows just what talents lie within their pupils, and are ever proud to find that individual golden key, nurture those talents and see them shared with a wider audience.

Of the many competitions entered into by schools today, public speaking – once out of fashion – proves especially popular with students, especially the opportunity to visit other schools, and the further a team goes in regional and national competitions, some quite splendid host locations. The wider life skills and personal confidence which public speaking develops are not to be underestimated. See pages 194–195 for an example.

- *Sport for all, excellence for some*

  Physical education merits a special mention, and not only because many (not all by any means) students nominate it as their favourite subject. The gym, the fitness room, the sports hall, the running track, the playing fields play a vital part in the education of children and young people.

  Teachers of physical education will tell you regularly how inspections and reviews of schools, while doing justice to English, mathematics and science, regularly fail to visit and celebrate PE. What the great PE classroom frequently evidences is strong peer leadership and modelling – gifted teachers able to model a badminton backhand or a Fosbury flop; teachers knowing when to coach closely and when to let go so the students can practise, fail wisely, and try again. Learning is about following a model, recall, repetition, trial and error – all writ large in the gymnasium.

  We all recognise just how difficult true differentiation is, and how in the wrong hands it can be used as a professional stick with which to beat teachers. What great physical education classrooms so often demonstrate is 'sport for all, excellence for some', in many ways a 'differentiation' ideal for all teachers to aspire to, irrespective of subject.

****

How ambitious can schools be in taking learning 'outdoors'?

Health and safety, safeguarding, budget preoccupation and the sheer logistics of travel in today's world are not to be underestimated. Yet where school leaders are enabling and facilitating, the great classroom can readily move beyond the interior four walls. Where thoughtfully integrated into weekly and termly planning – whatever the age group

– moving learning into external settings is viable and enriching. Highly skilled teachers have the confidence to lead such ventures and adventures into what is often slightly unknown and unpredictable territory. Feedback from students is invariably positive. 'Repeat, repeat, repeat' is their message.

ASIDE

National Trust: 50 things to do before you're 11¾ – and still great fun when you're 81¾

1. Get to know a tree.
2. Roll down a really big hill.
3. Camp outdoors.
4. Build a den.
5. Skim a stone.
6. Go welly wandering.
7. Fly a kite.
8. Spot a fish.
9. Eat a picnic in the wild.
10. Play conkers.
11. Explore on wheels.
12. Have fun with sticks.
13. Make a mud creation.
14. Dam a stream.
15. Go on a wintry adventure.

(The full list can be found at https://www.nationaltrust.org.uk/visit/50-things.)

Q. What equivalent kinds of listings and ambitions for the outdoors does your school have, for any ages?

PREPARATION

The singular double act that is teaching and learning is by its very nature an unwritten contract between teacher and learner, unless tutoring and other agencies are involved, in which case payment is being made and the contract becomes more formal.

The teacher

Accepting that teachers are paid professionals, the unwritten contract in classrooms is a de facto agreement that says: 'I as the teacher will plan, prepare and deliver high quality lessons. I as the learner will do all that I can to benefit from what is presented.' It is worth noting here that in schools and classrooms that are providing a poor education, there is little attempt by the teacher to challenge the pupils; in turn the pupils see little point in rising to any challenge placed in front of them.

In great classrooms there is also – sometimes written, sometimes unwritten, but always spoken – the expectation that for every hour the teacher and pupils spend together on their science or their history, the (more senior) learner will need to give a 'companion hour' outside the classroom by way of homework and independent study. That way lies success in recall, consolidation and practice of new skills and the cementing of fresh knowledge.

To enter any profession is to spend a period in training, in the case of teaching generally following a degree course followed by bespoke teacher training in one form or another. These years of preparation are just the beginning of a teaching career in which the preparation and planning of lessons, assemblies, in-service training and team meetings provide the diurnal round.

Practice probably never makes perfect; over time the accumulation of experience may render teaching a particular lesson slightly easier, though no two lessons are ever alike. Those new to schools often say that their first few years in the classroom are a relentless merry-go-round of lesson preparation, teaching, marking, planning, marking, teaching, recovery...

Lesson preparation is not about drilled sameness. I once asked a student in a senior classroom what the 'LO' on the board meant. He turned and said: 'It's only because you're here as the inspector that the LO is there – it never normally is.' Out of the mouths of babes, and probably not a common occurrence these days. That said, the slavish adherence to writing down the lesson objective at the start of every lesson has its downsides, and skilled teachers find creative ways of setting out the aims of a given lesson – and, on occasion, deliberately not setting down the outcome right at the outset.

Unquestionably, great classrooms are underpinned by planning and preparation of a high order. Early years practitioners base their curriculum planning in the three prime areas of learning and development: communication and language; personal, social, and emotional development; physical development. Specific areas of learning are literacy, mathematics, understanding the world, and expressive arts and design. And the characteristics of effective learning are: playing and exploring, active learning, creating and thinking critically.

That is a list which teachers of all age groups might reflect on, for it describes the foundation blocks of formal education.

All these come together in great early years classrooms through expert team planning of activities, tasks and outcomes, complemented by the creation of resources of all shapes and sizes to stimulate young minds. In great early years settings there truly is a sense of awe and wonder that children experience and that teachers, support staff and parents frequently comment upon. There are also clear and high expectations of children to play with purpose and learn with intent; this is achieved because of the high quality of the deliberate and individualised planning for every child as she or he works on their own, in groups or as a class.

Astutely guided independent learning is the hallmark of early years. That same degree of independent learning does not come again until post-16 (see diagram on page 151). Continuous provision in Key Stage 1, skilfully planned, extends valuably for many children that level of independence, and so too do many curriculum topics through the primary years.

In great primary classrooms, whether children are working on topics or themes, or focused on the science or maths national curriculum, or practising phonics, or working in the art room or sports hall – what is ever evident is how seamlessly pupils are joyfully focused, all rooted in the teachers' expert planning and preparation of appropriate resources. Early careers teachers often comment on how easy the experienced teacher makes it look. They are right: it looks easy; it isn't, but it comes with purposeful practice by the professional as he builds his expert repertoire, and constantly in collaboration with fellow teachers.

The secondary teacher's planning is significantly shaped by curriculum and examination syllabus coverage: knowing the subject content in detail and – through the teacher's own scholarship, skills and wider reading – enhancing classroom dialogue and interaction. At every turn, the teacher in a great secondary classroom is seeking to create a strong culture for learning, to pass on to pupils their passion for subject, to support all learners in mastering a new idea or skill, to ensure that time is well used – this cocktail is fundamentally rooted in the hours of preparation (including marking) that precede each lesson.

The extract on page 136 from *Thunder And Lightnings* is a delightful reflection on curriculum repetition from children's point of view. In the contemporary classroom in the UK there is a relentless attention to the intent, implementation and impact of what is taught. Great classrooms are attuned to the trinity of Is in an intelligent and selective way that means curriculum coverage is an engaging intellectual trampoline rather than a dull safety net, important though safety nets are.

The pupil

So where does all this 'go' go to? If the teacher is more than acquitting him or herself professionally, relishing their craft by inspiring the pupils, what is the pupils' active response?

In great classrooms there is always an explicit understanding of the current journey of learning: where it has been, where it now is, and where the journey is going. There is a shared understanding amongst teacher and pupils about why they are studying what they are studying, and why topics are sequenced in the way they are. This has always been a feature of the best classrooms, and in a way examination syllabuses lead this common appreciation of the order in which subject matter is being covered.

They then enjoy talking with their peers, parents and classroom visitors about their studies. Students especially come into their own when explaining the way in which they have created and polished a particular artefact in technology, a speech in drama, a model in history, or a TED Talk in biology.

In great classrooms, inspired by their teachers, students keep their part of the unwritten contract by ensuring they prepare well for a sequence of lessons through homework, independent study, wider reading and research. Pupils are to be seen before and after school in informal groups or in the library following up on something which is new to them; they are fascinated and captured by a particular formula or experiment and want to explore further. That spirit of enquiry is, in the end, sourced in the teacher's original fine planning.

A word on tests and examinations

The unwritten contract between teacher and learner is nowhere more in evidence than in preparing pupils for tests and examinations. To have qualified as a teacher means being pretty experienced in tests and examinations over a school and training career. Teachers are thus confident in preparing students for the demands exams present, whether at 11+ or 16+. And teachers who are also examiners for external bodies bring an invaluable extra dimension to their teaching and their schools.

In great classrooms teachers demonstrate considerable creativity and ingenuity to making revision sessions interesting in a way that facts and figures and theorems stick in young minds; they devise all kinds of mnemonics; they offer tips and study guides and extra lessons – all geared at maximising examination performance and top attainment. This is the bread and butter of upper secondary education and great teachers are properly proud to be judged by the results of their students. (See pages 193–194 for example.)

Coda. Watch any accomplished chef or decorator or tree surgeon in action: thorough preparation and planning are essential, time-consuming and pivotal to the successful completion of task. So too with the teacher, in any setting. Planning needs to bring professional enjoyment or it will weigh heavily. Each teacher develops her or his own ways of doing, yet equally recognises that there is great merit in planning in teams: crafting a first draft, sharing it with others, revising and adding interest – that way lies mutual professional fulfilment.

ASIDE

Teamwork – an apocryphal tale

There are four people named Everybody, Somebody, Anybody and Nobody. There was an important job to be done and Everybody was asked to do it. Everybody was sure Somebody would do it. Anybody could have done it, but Nobody did it.

Somebody got angry about that, because it was Everybody's job. Everybody thought Anybody could do it but Nobody realised that Everybody wouldn't do it. It ended up that Everybody blamed Somebody when Nobody did what Anybody could have done.

Q. Reflecting on the amusing dysfunction described above, what in your experience makes for effective team planning?

READING 5

A school lesson should be of the nature of a dramatic performance, from which some interest and amusement may be expected; while at the same time there must be solid and business-like work done. Variety of every kind should be attempted; the blackboard should be used, there should be some simple jesting, there should be some anecdote, some disquisition, and some allusion if possible to current events, and the result should be that the boys should not only feel that they have put away some definite knowledge under lock and key, but also that they have been in contact with a lively and more mature mind. Exactly in what proportion the cauldron should be mingled, and what its precise ingredients should be, must be left to the taste and tact of the teacher.

The Schoolmaster by Arthur Christopher Benson

QUESTIONS

Pushed to identify a singular feature of great classrooms, the posing of great questions might well come top of my list. It is not just the questions themselves, but the style in which they are posed and *how* students' responses are managed and built upon. What accomplished teachers do with the answers they receive is fascinating to observe.

Why do we use questions in our everyday lives: Why? What? Who? When? In essence, it is to receive answers to give us information we do not already possess. With when, who and what, it can often be a closed question to which there is a definite answer, helping us to do something, go somewhere or identify someone. But listen for a moment to a young child asking the question why? Why does my sister pull those faces? Why do we have to leave? Why is it raining?

Those more open questions are not so much about securing a definitive answer (although young children want clear answers and will repeat the question until they think they have a clear answer!), but are the beginnings of natural human wondering. In classrooms, teachers present factual information and then ask questions to check that new knowledge has been understood and can be recalled. Surface understanding leading to deeper learning is what is going on here. At a more sophisticated level, teachers begin to ask more searching questions to promote higher order thinking.

In early years, skilled teachers are asking: why is the water flowing quickly, why do these words rhyme, why do these numbers go in a sequence? As children move up through primary school, the teacher starts to work at a different level of sophistication: why do we use this mathematical formula here, why did peoples emigrate, why do we apply this fair test? And moving to older students, the questions become more demanding, with less obvious right and wrong answers: why (do we think) did this war leader act as he did, why did this character murder his wife, why did this painter use this technique, why not combine these two chemicals?

All such questions in classrooms are fundamentally aimed at helping children and students comprehend knowledge and skills that are new to them – or at least were recently new and the teacher is revisiting to ensure full understanding. We remember what we must think deeply about.

None of this questioning is possible without it being rooted in the teacher's own knowledge and skills base. Teachers are quick to recognise where they are working at the limits of their own knowledge, and in an information and digitally wealthy era can readily refer students to a reliable source for some answers. In great classrooms teachers demonstrate that their expert knowledge and skills rise out of them as easily as sap from a tree.

Visiting a Year 5 primary classroom it is usually easy to spot whether the teacher is the lead in the school for English or mathematics or science; we all lean into our comfort zones. That said, in the best primary schools, such is the quality of team planning that there is little sense of pupils not being extended by all teachers. Drop into a Year 9 history lesson and here again it will emerge whether the humanities teacher is first a geographer and second a historian – again, not always but usually. Move to a Year 12 physics class taught by a biologist, and it shows.

These observations are not to suggest that teachers cannot teach out of their subject comfort zones; indeed, many do so superbly. But it is to observe that really deep, provoking and ultimately illuminating questions are rooted in a teacher's own expert subject knowledge.

This is especially true when it comes to intellectual digression. A teacher secure in their own knowledge skin will not only allow but positively encourage pupils to wander off the subject, make connections beyond the classroom and offer apparently off-beam observations – all in the interest of embedding understanding, and certain that she will be able to pull ideas back together again rapidly and with common purpose.

So the posing of rich questions, rooted in teachers' own knowledge and planning related to the intended outcomes of the lesson, is a distinctive feature of great classrooms – and a teacher too is unafraid of unintended intellectual consequences once pupils' interests are sparked. To be in a classroom where highly skilled questioning is taking place is to be in a setting where scholarship, surprise and 'aha moments' punctuate proceedings.

The double act is truly at work here. How does the teacher *respond* to the questions she or he is posing? Certainly, the best classrooms *expect* students to respond in full phrases or sentences, well articulated – unless it's a Eureka moment demanding a one-word or one-figure answer. This student articulation is a given part of the rules of the game. And if time is being well orchestrated, then the teacher will not respond directly to the answer but engage other pupils – a few in turn – to build on the initial answer. 'Think about what you are going to say next' is a smart lead-in from the teacher to any whole-class discussion.

Too often in classrooms, there is a to-fro between the teacher and one pupil, and the opportunity is not taken to ensure that different pupils build upon the first answer before the teacher summarises and moves on.

The terms 'cold calling' and 'no hands up' frequently feature in whole-school teaching and learning policies. Too often in practice in classrooms there is shared confusion about what these policies mean in practice. In great classrooms there is real clarity and consistency as to whether, once a question is posed, pupils speak up instantly, raise their hand, or wait to be called on. In those classrooms, dialogue flows seamlessly between pupils and the teacher; where there is another adult in the classroom dialogue is enhanced by that adult's expertise.

The above paragraphs have focused on whole-class sessions; when working in smaller groups some of the identified pitfalls are less likely to occur. (See the Aside below.)

In great classrooms, how children work effectively in groups is carefully prepared for and scaffolded so that all learners make maximum progress. If roles of chair, scribe, observer, etc. are allocated, that is done with clarity and with purpose of outcome in mind so that time in groups is well used by each member. The skilled practitioner – whether with 7- or

17-year-olds, whether in a reading session or in a biology practical – ensures that everyone contributes, recognising that some students speak more readily than others, while some prefer to listen and comment occasionally.

Each of us learns in different ways, and great classrooms model that understanding of different styles of learning.

The Socratic tradition

Much of the thinking about questions and questioning in the Western tradition hails from the work of the Greek philosopher Socrates in the fifth century BC. The argument goes that the so-called Socratic Method is not 'teaching' per se; rather, it is 'enquiry'. Students are not passive recipients. The teacher leads by posing thought-provoking questions, and students engage by actively asking questions of their own. The discussion goes back and forth, demonstrating complexity and uncertainty rather than eliciting facts.

Clearly this Socratic technique, whilst applicable across the curriculum, is better adopted in some subject areas than others, which are rooted in more factual understanding. What I see in great classrooms is what I also come across when working with school leaders on self-evaluation. There is 'productive discomfort' based in that famous dictum of Socrates that 'the unexamined life is not worth living'.

ASIDE

Some teachers deal largely in questions, but if the class is large it needs almost genius to keep question and answer going with sufficient rapidity to ensure universal attention. Moreover, if the requisite enthusiasm is invoked, it requires a good deal of masterfulness to keep it within decorous bounds. I myself believe that questioning should be more used in small classes, and that with a large class a form of lecturing, interspersed with questions, is the more effective.

If a teacher has the gift of asking questions of a kind that stimulate curiosity by their form, and make the answering them into a brisk species of intellectual lawn-tennis, he is probably a very good teacher. But few men will probably have sufficient mental agility – and what is more, still fewer boys – and the result will be apt to be that the game will be played between the master and a few boys of some mental rapidity, and the majority of the class will have but a faint idea of what is going on.

The Schoolmaster by Arthur Benson, 1902

Q. Would you agree with Benson's key points here?

READING

My father still reads the dictionary every day. He says your life depends on your power to master words.

Arthur Scargill

An explicit focus on reading and accessing text is core to a successful classroom. Reading is the golden key to accessing the school curriculum and a lifetime's opportunities. Parental and wider social promotion of the reading habit weigh significantly.

Yet in our wealthy nation, with its long history of free education, we still have one in four of our 11-year-olds not meeting expected national standards in reading – and a similar percentage not achieving a grade 4 in English GCSE. And two years of interrupted schooling have certainly impacted reading standards, particularly for those children who find progress in reading hard to make.

The linguist Noam Chomsky identified that every human has an innate language acquisition device. Only in rare circumstances do humans not learn to speak, and this is true across cultures. The psychologist Steven Pinker remarks that while children are wired for sound, print is an optional accessory that must be painstakingly bolted on.

A UK political leader once said that the word 'priority' should not be used in the plural. In that spirit of just one priority for schools in relation to reading, we must break this cycle of a section of the young population growing up with faltering language skills. Let us be properly ambitious, set the goals and see where we get to.

- Every primary school to say to itself: almost all children will, at age 11+, have a reading age which matches at least their chronological age. And track reading ages from the early years to Year 6 in a joyously obsessional manner.
- Every secondary school to say to itself: no matter the child's starting point, almost all will achieve a grade 4 in English at 16+. And track reading ages from Year 7 to Year 11 in a joyously obsessional manner.

****

EXAMPLE 1

The county of Essex established the Year of Reading 2022–2023 with a £1 million investment and with these ambitions and aims.

EVERY ESSEX CHILD A CONFIDENT READER

Ambitions

Renewal: to support children and young people who have fallen behind with their reading over the past year.

Equality: to read confidently is the golden key to being a successful learner.

Ambition: to ensure that every Essex child leaves school able to read at their age level or better.

Aims

1. To encourage every community across the county to promote the importance of reading.
2. To encourage every family to enjoy reading together.
3. To encourage businesses, large and small across Essex, to promote the fun and joy of reading.

****

EXAMPLE 2

The county of East Sussex seconded a group of teachers to produce *The East Sussex Way*, excellently researched materials focusing on transition between primary and secondary. The trinity of oracy, reading and vocabulary is central. The booklet is available online here: https://blinks. education/TheEastSussexWay.

The *Contents* of the publication are as follows:

> *Section One*: Oracy at the point of transition
>
> Case Study 1: Creating talk-rich learning
>
> Case Study 2: Starting Year 7 history with a talk-centred approach
>
> *Section Two*: Reading at the point of transition
>
> Case Study 1: Better reading partnership
>
> Case Study 2: Supporting reading through Bedrock vocabulary
>
> Case Study 3: Teaching to reading ages
>
> *Section Three*: Vocabulary at the point of transition
>
> Case Study 1: Explicit teaching of vocabulary
>
> Case Study 2: Command vocabulary
>
> Case Study 3: Promoting academic vocabulary
>
> *Appendix 1*: Strategies to encourage high quality peer-to-peer exploratory talk
>
> *Appendix 2*: Practical strategies for enhancing vocabulary.

****

All schools and all classrooms – irrespective of subject content – need to commit to this central ambition that every child reads at least in line with their reading age, and be *joyously obsessive* about realising that ambition. This must include the meticulous tracking of all pupils' reading ages as they move up through the years. We often complicate matters in schools rather than adopting a 'less is more' approach with clarity and razor-like focus.

So, what's to do?

Since reading the Bullock Report in 1975 and its fundamental recommendation that every teacher should be a teacher of English, I have dreamt that secondary schools should suspend their English departments for a period. All English teachers would go on a two-year sabbatical, only for them to return to find that *other* subject teachers have made them redundant, such is their daily relish in the teaching of the English language.

In the meantime, with hearts and minds, let the entire system implement the following with whole-school consistency and, vitally, involve implementation and commitment not just by teachers of English and literacy but by all staff. In secondary schools in particular, the history of cross-curricular initiatives is not a proud one, bedevilled by subject empires. Of course, strong departments with a passion for their subjects lie at the heart of great schools. But altruism and self-interest need to collide so that, reaching for the Holy Grail, *all* secondary teachers see themselves as teachers of the English language.

Primary and special schoolteachers naturally do see themselves in that way; even they need to place greater emphasis on this golden key.

An easy reading agenda

First, schools need a rigorous approach to word recognition: enabling children to use a phonetic approach, to divide words into syllables for pronunciation, to have a knowledge of prefixes and suffixes.

Second, a planned approach to vocabulary development: learning new words, keywords and concepts, technical abbreviations and etymology, symbols and formulae – through regular and consistent use of a dictionary and a thesaurus.

Third, a systematic engagement with comprehension and organisation of text: reading to self and reading aloud, summarising what has been read, distinguishing essential from non-essential, fact from opinion, drawing inferences and conclusions, noting cause and effect, reading between the lines.

Fourth, a programme to promote reading interests: voluntary reading for pleasure, reading for personal information, developing a passion for particular subjects, the use of the school library, audio-recordings, the downloading onto the iPad or Kindle of a favourite biography.

Fifth, a whole-school approach to study skills: sitting still long enough to read, using skimming for different purposes, reading maps and graphs, learning how to take notes, reading more rapidly with adequate comprehension, forming the study habit.

Reflecting on the five points above, skilled practitioners will not make the mistake of adopting simply an age-related approach to the teaching of reading. Rather, they will select what works for a given child or group of children at a particular point in their reading journey. Fluency is the goal. Teachers and tutors must be driven by the belief that every child can tackle texts with confidence, whether on the printed page or on the Kindle.

Reading silently, reading aloud, reading around the class, reading for pleasure, reading for information: the imperative of reading across the curriculum lies at the heart of great classrooms.

From early years' irresistible book tents to themed book corners in every primary classroom; from the poster promotion of books in primary and secondary corridors and common spaces; from telephone boxes and buses in playgrounds where books are swapped and talked about; from subject mini-libraries in secondary classrooms to the learning resource centre, ably supported by the school librarian; from sixth-form study centres lined with subject periodicals to learning zones where digital access to text is so easy – *all* these add up to a glorious 'more than the sum of their parts' to promote the reading habit.

ASIDE

What do we see in the best English lessons which can be features of every lesson to promote reading, vocabulary and oracy?

- Pupils being expected to answer questions in developed phrases rather than just monosyllables, from early years onwards

- Teachers giving more time for pupils to develop fuller oral responses to questions posed
- Teachers enabling pupils to pose questions of one another, in order that pupils practise their sounds and speech patterns
- Direct and regular correction from staff in how children speak and pronounce their letters, and in how they hold a pencil/pen and form their letters
- Structured and regular drama/acting opportunities in which children and students are expected to project their voices and practise speaking at length with good eye contact: TED Talks.
- Regular use of limericks, couplets, verses, short poems being set to be learned by heart and for recitation in groups; parents can be involved in this
- Consistent use of established EAL techniques (pattern, repetition, consolidation, elaboration) with children whose *first* language is English
- Regular use of short dictations, across the curriculum, with an emphasis on keen listening and high quality presentation of writing. See pages 179–181.

Q. What do you see in the best lessons to promote fluency in oral and written language? What would you add?

Note: ideas and themes around language covered in this chapter are picked up again in Zoon on page 159.

SCHOLARSHIP

Try this: ask a 16-year-old student what the meaning of the word 'scholarship' is. Chances are they will tell you it is something they can apply for to support their education at a top institution. Its etymology – with roots in Greek and Latin *scholaris* (of a school) and later in the 14th century 'a scholar, a learned person having great knowledge of philosophy and classical literature' – has been lost over time. Or rather its meaning has been refashioned over time, such is the bendability of the English language.

At the heart of great classrooms is the inspiring teacher who has a passion for their subject and for how children learn. Great teachers want to find the golden key in every child which awakens his or her interest and aptitudes. Ask any group of pupils, from age 7 to 17, what makes for enjoyable classroom learning, and they talk about the teacher who loves their subject and shares that passion with their students. The development and promotion of real scholarship matters.

Children and students are infected by the enthusiasms of their teachers. They deeply respect the teacher who has a breadth and depth of knowledge that they can, at their age, only dream of and aspire to. Just think for a moment of the teachers you remember with affection from you own schooldays...

Yes, it will be a teacher who knew and valued you as a person. It is likely also that it was a mathematician, a biologist, a linguist or a musician whose own memorable scholarship was not in doubt, who shared their ambitions and enthusiasms.

In an early years context 'scholarship' is embodied in those expert teachers and other adults who deeply understand child development and know how to educate ('lead out') children so that they flourish as young human beings. In great early years classrooms, adults are quite simply, in the words of Guy Holloway, 'building brains'; they are keenly focused on the social, moral, intellectual and physical development of individual children whom they know so well. They plan magical resources to enable children to engage in *purposeful play* that develops their fine and gross motor skills, their social awareness, their thinking powers, their linguistic and mathematical awakenings. That's scholarship with young children.

I am fond of saying that early education is as simple and as complex as enabling children to do three things confidently and with joy – Sing, Share, Skip: in loco parentis plus! What lies behind developing those three skills is at the heart of great early years classrooms, indoors and outdoors.

Primary practitioners display their scholarship, yes, in continuing to know how to secure the best from a child; their knowledge of child development remains key. At the same time, they are using their passions and knowledge of subject matter across the curriculum to inspire young minds. It might appear at times that primary colleagues are expected to be Renaissance scholars, such is the demand on their cross-curricular subject knowledge.

Enter a Year 4 classroom and gaze in admiration at the artefacts and high quality writing which have been produced from children's authoritative research into the Egyptians. Step along the corridor to see the equivalent depth of learning across the curriculum in Year 5 studying the Tudors. Travel next to Year 6, whose written and oral responses to World War One poets is humbling.

All those outcomes are sourced in the teacher's own research, knowledge and passion for subject: what I call 'scholarship' in contemporary great classrooms. And this links fundamentally to building pupils' cultural capital, their encountering 'the best that has been thought and said' in whatever culture they are living in. Of course, what matters is teachers themselves being able to bring what C.P. Snow termed 'the two cultures' of the arts and the sciences to every classroom. Excellent curriculum planning seen in schools today helps realise that ambition.

In great classrooms secondary subject experts have scholarship oozing out of their pores. It is that passion for subject which has probably brought them into teaching in the first place *and* that professional urge to share what they know with young minds. Further maths students exploring the square root of −1; A level geographers studying earthquake patterns; IB bilingual students presenting 'les informations' and 'the news' simultaneously – you know you are in the presence of great minds, enabled by the scholarship of their teachers.

Digressions

I once asked a group of so-called gifted and talented 14-year-olds to draw images of what made for effective and less effective lessons. Intriguingly, they set out on their sugar paper to draw a series of expanding and contracting heads.

The more effective a lesson became, they charted with their colour pens, the larger the students' heads and the smaller the teacher's head.

It was a vivid series of images that has stayed with me. They were seeking to point out that the teacher begins the lines of enquiry, giving space for students to continue the journey.

Of course, the well-prepared teacher enters the classroom with clear plans and lesson objectives and intentions in mind. Equally, the confident teacher will rightly take the pupils on a magical mystery tour, taking their learning into unknown territories, before reassuringly returning to base camp. The most stimulating TED Talks do just that.

It is the accomplished teacher, comfortable in his or her own knowledge of subject matter, who is able to master and manage digression – digression indeed that may be student led. To watch creative digression that builds on pupils' previous knowledge and dares them to think differently is to watch fine learning.

Join a Year 6 teacher who is reading *The Boy in the Striped Pyjamas* and see how adroitly he fields the most challenging of divergent questions *and* how he supports those pupils struggling emotionally with the novel's content. Or be party to an A level history seminar wrestling with the difference between freedom fighters and terrorists – everyone has strong views – where the teacher harnesses her considerable knowledge of Gandhi, Mandela and Guevara to present objective evidence upon which students can make a judgement.

High quality, probing, Socratic questioning, which presents both surprise and scholarship, is a joy to observe and is unfailingly motivational to the learner.

To teach is to learn

It is a truism that many of us learn something fully once we are called upon to teach some knowledge or a skill to someone else. How often have you found yourself nodding along in agreement as something practical like mending a dripping tap is explained to you, only to find you haven't really 'got it' once you call upon yourself to fix it? And always beware the 'expert' who shows you, in the blink of an eye, how to perform some function on a new piece of equipment, then leaves you marooned with the instruction booklet in various languages, but not your own!

I see children from the earliest ages presenting topics to one another, skilfully nurtured by the teacher. This arises from teachers who know what true independent learning means, know how to create it, and know how to manage it in the best interests of all learners.

Best practice is certainly rooted in the teacher who expects, from time to time, to talk and do less than her students. She details how – in the course of the following week and sharing her lessons plans with students – one pair will lead the lesson starter, another will lead the mini-plenary, and yet another will conclude the lesson. In the upper secondary years, this leads to young women and men – not many years away from such expectations in further and higher education – teaching their peers the intricacies of advanced level chemistry or aspects of linguistics.

One final image of scholarship: a class of Year 10 students studying waves as part of a GCSE geography lesson.

The teacher sits at the visualiser and draws various sea wave movements with delicacy and attention to detail, drawing forth from the class – as they draw with him in their books – their ideas on why waves move in different ways on different shorelines. The class conclude with this video of surfing off Nazare, Portugal, where the largest underwater canyon in Europe allows the swell to form perfect giant waves – a wonderful example of teaching and learning moving out of the classroom window to bring a topic alive.

https://www.youtube.com/watch?v=GJc4Ir78KdE – Watch it! The students who did flew high in their examination answers on this topic.

ASIDE

Aim high

One 3–19 international school affirms that confident children, with a love of learning and intellectual curiosity, can:

- make sense of and deal creatively and positively with the circumstances of their lives, their current environment and the world at large
- command language in its major forms and use them readily, competently and easily to serve their purposes
- master one other major international language in addition to their heritage tongue
- learn to think, respond and behave according to the form and conventions of major disciplines; that is, they are able where required to act as scientists, historians, geographers, technologists and mathematicians would
- command essential learning skills: they are comfortable with and can use modern technologies to suit their learning purposes
- respond to the creative and expressive arts in a way which enlarges personal awareness and creative and learning potential, refines sensibility and sensitivity, and provides for spiritual development
- problem-solve: they can engage with and bring reason and practical resource to bear on the challenges and problems of human existence

- go on learning in a progressive way, building on what they have acquired and mastered, and impelled by an abiding sense of curiosity
- demonstrate a strong moral and ethical sense and the capacity to relate sympathetically with others
- exercise a critical faculty which enables them to distinguish between the substantial and the trivial, the genuine and the spurious, and to identify the crucial points in argument, data, literature and presentation.

Q. Which of these in your experience characterises students with a love of learning?

TIME

The ancient Greeks had two understandings of time, *chronos* and *kairos*. Both are important, but the latter rarely gets the attention it warrants.

Chronos time is chronological time: how we measure our days and our lives quantitatively. We've been setting our lives by some form of chronological time for centuries. Judging by our cultural lexicon – 'Time waits for no one', 'Time is of the essence', 'Time is money' – then we are afraid of losing it.

Perhaps we should also look at things through the prism of *kairos*.

How do we honour *kairos* time, what the Greeks understood as the most opportune time for something new? The concept has its origins in the practice of Greek archery, representing the moment when the archer finds the perfect opening to shoot his arrow and hit the target. Kairos was also the Greek god of opportunity. He had wings on his feet and darted about swiftly.

Great classrooms embody both of these concepts of time in meeting the needs of pupils. They are places equally where every minute counts and where no opportunity for new learning is missed.

A question I am fond of asking groups of pupils – in any part of the world and in whatever kind of school – is this: 'In an average 50-minute session, how much learning would you say goes on?' Answers are always instructive and offer a pretty reliable snapshot of how well time is used across the curriculum and at different times of the day. The most memorable answer to the question came from a group of 12-year-olds who wittily observed that in one 50-minute lesson from a particular teacher they received an *hour* of learning every time, such was their sense of how effectively the teacher planned and delivered her lesson.

So, what are the constituent features of great classrooms where both *chronos* and *kairos* are valued equally?

Chronos time used profitably

From the moment students enter the classroom there are clear expectations that the following 50 or 100 minutes will be profitably used by the pupils. That constructive use of time is rooted in the teacher's planning: a 50-minute session demands a different kind of orchestration from one of 100 minutes.

The lesson may begin with a short quiz to recap on the last lesson; a short discussion on homework, promptly collected in; a 'fix-it' 10 minutes correcting a previous piece of work; a short video to pique pupils' imagination; a reference to the earlier assembly and its celebration of a particular achievement; reflections on a sobering piece of the day's news to kick-start study – the possibilities are wonderfully wide-ranging. I once arrived at a Year 10 geography lesson with the students: on arrival we were given a card with notes on it which sent us to different parts of the classroom for research on features of melting glaciers; it proved a highly motivating start to the session.

An appropriate and well-adjusted pace to lessons is a feature of great classrooms. Transitions are managed in such a way that little time is lost – a feature of early years and primary classrooms in particular. Where students are moving between individual, pair and group work, here again clear expectation, strong planning and everyone aware of purpose make up the key ingredients for time being used intentionally.

When the class is brought together for a few moments to update peers on what they are doing and thinking, and the teacher may draw out some salient pointers for next steps in learning – this is done with sharp focus, no nonsense, and collective understanding that 'we have got this far, now let's move on'. This is not about a rush but about a shared sense of purpose and achievement in the precious time available.

Secondary schools can be places 'where nothing ever gets finished', as one Year 7 girl observed when I asked her at the end of her first term in secondary school about comparisons with Year 6. Further, one tell-tale sign of this aspect is scanning through secondary pupils' books and reading the familiar teacher comment 'please finish this work'.

Students regularly talk about great classrooms as being places where teachers are fair, strict and 'give us time to think'. Teachers are always under pressure to cover the content, in inspection-speak to move from intent to impact. Yet great classrooms marry that content coverage with giving important space for mini-plenaries and pauses during which new knowledge can be embedded, new skills rehearsed and consolidated. A homework may also have been set seamlessly at a certain timely point.

It is in physical education, science, and drama – to take three examples – where the teacher 'lets go' and students lead learning, that one frequently observes time being very effectively deployed as students move between activities, making notes, encouraging and correcting their peers, sharing practices, buzzing with the progress they are making, the results they are achieving and, not infrequently in science, the failures of the experiments and 'what we should have done differently'. Failing wisely is always an important part of learning, and skilled teachers make sure time is set aside to reflect on where things have not turned out successfully.

Whatever journey the lesson in any subject has taken the children on, the final 5 to 10 minutes in great classrooms are sacrosanct.

The teacher may have allowed and encouraged pupils to pursue instructive and entertaining digressions, but will have set aside time to recap, pause, recap and check that everyone understands the key outcomes of the session. On many, many occasions pupils will ask the teacher if they can revisit a particular hard-to-grasp idea when next the class convenes; the teacher notes this with alacrity and also offers to see pupils outside the lesson if they want that little bit of extra support.

This final section of the lesson is frequently used in great classrooms to ask the simple and telling question of pupils: 'what do you know/can you do now that you didn't/couldn't when you entered the room?' In safe and mutually trusting environments, where there is no fear of failure, it's a quick gauge for the teacher, and allows her to reassure where the next lesson will pick up the story. And, as in all great stories, children have a sense of where the plot is going, but are not altogether sure of how the characters will get there nor the travails and triumphs they'll encounter on the way.

Kairos time: opportunities taken and missed

As a teacher consumed by the everyday commerce of the classroom, taking the register and reporting absences, preoccupied by getting the planning right, preparing the resources, knowing the pupils, marking their books – there is every pressure imaginable to want to 'press on' with curriculum coverage. Great classrooms recognise all this and still find time to seize opportunities for divergent thinking and digression which emerge from the students.

As an observer in classrooms it is easy to spot an opportunity in learning missed: early years practitioners are especially expert at seeing *in the moment* a child wanting to explore something in a particular direction – and at that age time allows. Further up the school system when – in poet Wordsworth's words – 'the shades of the prison-house begin to close upon the growing boy', too often a pondering or a question posed by a student is passed by in the interests of 'moving on'. It is ever a challenging balance for the teacher.

Skilled teachers, with excellent antennae for their pupils' current thinking, seek to hear that pondering and question when clearly related to the mathematical, scientific, linguistic matter in hand. Or, if they think it really is a cul-de-sac for today, that hanging question may well become next week's lesson, homework or wider research topic. All easier said than done, but a hallmark of the best classrooms is that they never lose sight of *kairos* time.

****

Returning to *chronos*: time *is* money, time *is* of the essence – children get one go at this thing called school. Sociologist Michael Rutter wrote a seminal book titled *Fifteen Thousand Hours*, to draw attention to the number of hours that children spend in school between the ages of 4 and 16, and to highlight the considerable impact that schools make in the 'nature versus nurture' debate.

As a secondary headteacher I used to say to the deputy responsible for the timetable that hers was the most important job in the school. Think about it for a moment: the lives of 1,200 students and 100+ staff, 190 days a year, 6 hours a day. Do the maths. That's a lot of time to play with. How a school timetable and day are constructed shapes feelings, moods and dispositions towards learning, whether for 5- or 15-year-olds.

Great classrooms take very seriously the orchestration of time within lessons, and the management of time over weeks and terms. Children's fulfilled days at school depend on it.

And – importantly – everyone needs to rest from time to time, to restore batteries, to live to enjoy another day, indeed to reflect on oneself as a professional. A few reflections from another age below.

ASIDE

I do not believe that it is a fair thing to one's profession to work too hard in the holidays. The temptation is great to an ardent sightseer to travel feverishly about and to try and press a great deal into the time; the man who is interested in literary work is apt to immerse himself in writing; the philanthropist or the evangelist is inclined to study problems, or to make his voice heard in the pulpit. But though the main thing is that the holidays should be spent in a congenial way, it is a bad thing to feel that the coming term is an interruption of one's real preferences...

There is no sadder or more deadening thing than to go back to a profession which bores you, without interest or zeal, unless, indeed, you are in the unhappy position of having neither enthusiasm nor preferences; and in this case it is not even conscientious to pursue, unwillingly and heavily, a profession on which the minds and characters and fortunes of so many human beings depend.

The Schoolmaster by Arthur Benson, 1902

UNDERSTUDIES

'understudy' *noun*

– (in the theatre) a person who learns another's role in order to be able to act at short notice in their absence

One thought to begin: should we think about renaming those who assist in classrooms as 'understudies'? Why keep it as a word preserved for the theatre when it is a pretty fair description of teaching and learning assistants in any context?

If an army marches on its proverbial stomach, schools march on the generous range of support they receive from those who don't teach but who contribute in many directions, and without whom the place called school could not flourish. As a headteacher for 15 years in three different schools, I had a number of idiosyncratic practices which evolved over the years, but one I held firmly to. Every Friday afternoon I would visit classrooms across the school accompanied by a member of the administration and sites team.

The two-fold purpose was to cheer myself up before the weekend *and* to point out to the finance or admissions officer something or someone in classrooms that their actions had impacted upon. The weekly visits with different colleagues, who often did not move out of their behind-the-scenes offices, helped them to see how integral they were to the workings and well-being of the school community.

Great classrooms cannot operate successfully without the good offices of 'non-teaching' staff, a phrase that is still in common parlance, but probably ought not to be. 'Understudy' is much better.

It is worth comparing the teaching profession here with the medical profession. Spend any time in a mid-size general practitioners' surgery today: the doctors remain a central feature of medical care, but they are surrounded by a team of nurses, nutritionists, physiotherapists, auxiliaries. Visit a busy hospital and the same is true: a veritable army of medical and administrative personnel rushed off their feet to focus on patients' needs. And if it has been your fortune to be wheeled into an operating theatre, you will have glimpsed a team of gowned players about to get to work on you.

Classrooms do not usually have teams of adults other than teachers (AOTs), but in special schools, for example, there may well be four adults for a class of eight students, depending on pupils' severity of needs. Special schools which focus on speech and language will commonly have the teacher, the speech therapist and a teaching assistant to support 15 children.

In any school, and certainly in great classrooms, the role of the expert teacher is paramount. How that teacher deploys teaching and learning assistants is critical. Whole-school policies and practices usually govern how AOTs are spread across a school, and where those practices have been thought through intelligently, the impact on individuals and groups of pupils is significant.

In early years settings, it is sometimes difficult to know who is the teacher and who is the 'understudy' as the adults work seamlessly together as 'key workers' for different groups of children. The presence of adults who are bilingual in the heritage tongues of the children can be especially supportive, and those with a training in speech and language bring a further bonus.

Planning and supervising children indoors and outdoors as they move between activities is the bread and butter of the early years practitioner, and in great classrooms it is the adults' strong mutual understanding of roles that shines through. To walk-and-talk in a large school through a number of nursery and Reception learning spaces with the early years lead is to enjoy an animated and irrepressible conversation about these vital years when young brains are built.

Throughout primary schools, well-briefed adults other than teachers play a vital role. In the best classrooms, their own good subject knowledge and strong interpersonal skills are apparent, and the way in which they complement the teacher's role gives those classrooms something extra. At best, it is accomplished co-teaching that one observes. The lexicographer Dr Johnson, when asked 'what is poetry?', observed that 'it is much easier to say what it is not'. The same might be said of teaching assistants: you certainly know quickly when their practice is less effective, usually measured in children being noisy rather than buzzy.

In the secondary context, great classrooms include assistants who play an integral part in the planning, are well briefed by the teacher and are involved in whole-school training opportunities to advance their own subject and pedagogical knowledge. Science, art, design technicians – with their own practical skills and subject knowledge which may be different from the teacher's – are frequent and welcome contributors to lessons and can have a decisive impact in helping unlock a student's understanding.

The word 'understudy' leads this chapter. In so many ways it is a word from the theatre which can best describe many adults other than teachers who, when needed, do step into the teacher's shoes if she is absent for any reason. In great classrooms, those understudies step seamlessly into that role, and as they are known and respected by pupils the good commerce of the lesson can continue purposefully.

Further, when thoughtfully planned together, the assistant can provide useful feedback to the teacher on how particular tasks and activities are or are not meeting the needs of all students. This is professional development at its best – in the moment, and nuancing and reconfiguring classroom practice in the best interests of the students.

(Accomplished so-called 'cover supervisors' add a significant dimension to a school's daily well-being, for teachers and students alike. And successful schools have thought differently and creatively about 'cover' in today's digital environment, improving the pupils' classroom experiences, removing any need for external agency staff and making important budget savings.)

A word on inclusion

Teachers and support staff can change the lives of all children, but particularly those from less educationally supportive backgrounds and those who find learning difficult. We know in any walk of life that achieving success serves to motivate us further. For children and young people 'on the margins' it is with communication and language, social interaction and relationships, and with improving learning that schools can make a real difference.

Great classrooms harness the skills of assistants to ensure all pupils are included, whatever their individual learning needs. AOTs can help shape the attitudes to learning of a disengaged child, making a real difference to the overall well-being and flow of the classrooms. Their kindness, care and attention to detail with those children can be make or break to successful inclusion. Certainly, the most effective 'understudies' learn from their teachers, have rigorously high expectations of every child they work with, *and* create that space to nurture an individual whose social and emotional needs at a given moment require that extra bit of attention and empathy.

A school community advances handsomely when teachers and adults in a range of support roles train and plan together for the common purpose of accelerating pupils' learning and promoting a whole-school climate of ambition and diverse achievements.

ASIDE

Addressing disadvantage – traps to avoid

1. Less affluent pupils and families don't value education and have low aspirations.
2. Less affluent families aren't interested in how their child is performing academically or socially.
3. Low number of disadvantaged pupils in a school = low priority.

4. Schools can solve all the social problems children face.

5. Assuming disadvantage is static.

6. Presuming disadvantaged children have poor vocabulary.

7. Over-intervention and withdrawal from classrooms. Presuming disadvantaged children have poor vocabulary.

8. Over-intervention and withdrawal from classrooms.

9. Progress is more important than attainment.

10. Activity must mean impact.

11. Trying to prove initiatives/interventions have worked quickly...

(For further reading, see https://researchschool.org.uk/unity/news/addressing-educational-disadvantage-in-schools-and-colleges-the-essex-way.)

Q. Which of the above do you recognise? Which of these has your school perhaps fallen into or challenged robustly?

READING 6

'Miss Beale said you would show me round, to look at the projects,' said Andrew.

'Why, do you want to copy one?' asked Victor, lifting a strand of hair and exposing one eye. 'You could copy mine, only someone might recognise it. I've done that three times already.'

'Whatever for?' said Andrew. 'Don't you get tired of it?'

Victor shook his head and his hair.

'That's only once a year. I did that two times at the junior school and now I'm doing that again,' he said. 'I do fish, every time. Fish are easy. They're all the same shape.'

'No, they're not,' said Andrew.

'They are when I do them,' said Victor. He spun his book round, with one finger, to show Andrew the drawings. His fish were not only all the same shape, they were all the same shape as slugs.

Thunder and Lightnings by Jan Mark

VIRTUAL

'virtual' *noun*

– created by computer technology and appearing to exist but not existing in the physical world

And even this dictionary definition is in flux...

When our environment changes we must adapt to survive and flourish. Across private, public and not-for-profit sectors coming out of 'lockdown', everyone looked at their historic ways of doing and asked themselves quite reasonably:

- What do we keep?
- What do we refresh?
- What do we ditch?

The enforced period of working at home for much of the population during the height of the COVID-19 health crisis has led to significant social change in how, where, and when people choose to work, rest and play. Societies across the world have been affected: the way people balance their working, leisure and family hours has been brought into sharp focus. And there is probably no going back.

The Economist Intelligence Unit published a teaching report in 2020 which laid stark some quite sobering data, cutting across key aspects of curriculum and assessment. Further, the data raise fundamental questions about the nature of the current examination system with its Luddite preoccupation with terminal written examinations.

- 28% only of respondents think their training has equipped them for managing stress and burnout, a leading cause of teacher shortages

- 38% only feel their training is equipping them to use digital technology
- 60% think new teachers will increase the use of technology by 2030
- 50% predict they will focus more on teaching social values and diversity, with an increased focus on social and emotional learning
- 90%+ agreed that the purpose of education must shift to helping students know how to collect, interpret and apply information, rather than just learning it.

The extraordinary becomes the commonplace, at a faster and faster rate. As a member of the School Curriculum & Assessment Authority in the 1990s I recall working on the IT National Curriculum and commenting to colleagues that the moment it is published, it will be out of date. And it was.

Such is the pace of change in the virtual world that I write this chapter in the certain knowledge that my words will date rapidly. How long before the smartphone is a smarterphone, the iPad an EyePad?

Just five years ago, commentators wrote about the FAANGs, an acronym referring to the stocks of the five most popular and best performing American technology companies: Facebook, Amazon, Apple, Netflix and Google. Facebook has become Meta, Google has become Alphabet and is under threat from OpenAI, and Netflix is undergoing fundamental review.

Lenin got it right when he said that there are decades when nothing happens, and weeks where decades happen. The words 'virtual' and 'blended' entered the educational vocabulary almost overnight when schools around the world were forced to close for everyday business in the early months of 2020 – and much has since been written about the social and educational impact of the 'lockdown'.

What have great classrooms taken from that period? What are the legacies and lessons learned which are in evidence today in emerging best practice?

Pedagogy

- The use of AI – from Century Tech to Microsoft Reader – has been integrated into teaching and learning, facilitating real-time assessment and a more personalised experience for students.

- The development of recursive feedback through platforms such as Parlay and Peer Scholar: pupils are used to communicating and collaborating online through social media and gaming, and these platforms enable a similar approach to peer feedback.
- Home–school and student–teacher interactivity have taken a significant leap; Teams and Seesaw were in place pre-COVID, but the way they are being used is much improved.
- Pupils, from an early age, producing podcasts and short films as part of their studies is commonplace.
- The production of many excellent tutoring resources – locally, regionally, nationally – for pupils to work on at home, with a particular focus on support for disadvantaged youngsters.
- E-safety: from developing safeguarding protocols for online visitors to tightening protocols and procedures for recording lessons and setting up online groups – schools are better for it.
- Teachers visiting each other's online lessons has enabled high quality conversations about curriculum content and styles of learning.

Ways of working

- Groups of schools are working more closely than ever before. The quality of communication and collaboration is significantly improved.
- Infrastructure – hardware and software – has seen major investments.
- EdTech coaches have been appointed and wise investment made in professional development to upskill staff.
- Online interviews, interactive training workshops, team meetings, parent interviews, global CPD opportunities are now embedded in schools' regular practice.
- Enhanced awareness of staff and pupils' mental health and well-being has brought many benefits to school communities.
- One important negative: teachers are drawn into time-consuming follow-up with students and families when out-of-school WhatsApp and other social media lead to argument and fractured relationships.

The promise of what Artificial Intelligence will deliver for society as a whole is just beginning to surface in schools. There is much debate about the perils of the likes of ChatGPT and DALL-E and quite strong reaction from educators concerned as never before about essays being written not by students but by intelligent robots. Yet the workload with marking that teachers and tutors have every week might just be lessened through such cutting-edge technologies. We shall hear more from the Institute for Ethics in AI (https://www.oxford-aiethics.ox.ac.uk/).

A recent survey of teenagers reported Roblox, Snapchat, TikTok and Instagram as websites where teenagers felt unsafe. Social media including these and other brands yet to be created are here to stay – and access to them comes at a younger and younger age. Great classrooms are learning to live with this helter-skelter of new technologies, its threats and opportunities.

The global pandemic as it profoundly affected schools may well in time be remembered in the words of Charles Dickens as 'the worst of times' and, in the most unintended ways, 'the best of times'. Before the pandemic, the challenge for great classrooms was finding the sweet spot between theoretical and experiential learning. Following the move to virtual learning, the quest for that sweet spot is intensifying, to the benefit of pupils and teachers with regard to both the content and styles of learning for the 21st century.

ASIDE

The learning scientist

The evidence arising out of the first global pandemic in a social media age is that students are dissatisfied with their online learning experience: the transition from 'brick' to 'click' has proven to be a challenge for many educators. More emphasis will need to be placed on educators to deliver in a multi-modal setting.

The higher level cognitive functions of Bloom's taxonomy – creating, evaluating, analysing and applying – involve the cortical areas responsible for decision making, association and motivation.

As automation continues to redefine the world of work it is critical that teachers can develop higher order thinking skills in learners; and support the development of intrinsic motivation for lifelong learning and the resilience required to navigate the unpredictability of modern life.

The future role of a teacher will surely be that of a learning scientist.

Cameron Mirza

Q. Do you agree with this analysis? What might you add in the light of your own experiences of virtual/blended teaching and learning?

WHOLE-SCHOOL

At the beating heart of all schools are the classrooms, their very raison d'être. To visit a two-classroom school in Nepal, or a four-classroom school in Pune, or indeed to visit a small rural primary in Suffolk with its two classrooms in the old schoolhouse and the schoolmaster's house adjacent – all these are a reminder that schools come into being with a focus on a space where children and teachers are brought together to learn.

Indeed, it worth reflecting that deschoolers/unschoolers (see the writings of Ivan Illich and John Holt) are yet to break through significantly anywhere in the world. Various movements have been launched, and while there are significant numbers of families who choose to home educate their children in many societies, there is something special about the place called school wherever you are on the globe. The floating schools operating 24/7 in the rural archipelagos of Indonesia are worth Googling, a vivid reflection of the universal hunger for education.

Research and common sense tell us that no school system is better than its teachers and those who lead the schools. It is as simple and complex as that when reflecting on top quality education in any context and with any age range.

Let us take leaders first.

The vast majority of school leaders have spent their 10,000+ hours in classrooms as teachers – and those experiences run through them like writing through a stick of rock. They remain teachers at heart in the same way that the very best teachers remain children at heart.

The best leaders are incorrigibly optimistic, regularly sharing compelling stories with staff about what has been achieved and will be achieved by everyone working collaboratively and with a common purpose. They are accomplished communicators. Just as teachers give well-rehearsed talks to students about their potential, effective leaders are restless for excellence *and* realistic about delivery.

How do the best leaders define and model excellence in their organisations and settings?

Headteachers and principals are clear that their organisation should be an employer of first choice, with working conditions and professional development opportunities the best they can be within financial and operational limits. They know that first and foremost teaching is a people business.

They are ambitious that their school should be a first choice for families – that no parents push a buggy, cycle or drive past their school gates to travel to another setting – and that no students hop on a bus to avoid their local school.

Leaders are united in their ambition to create environments for learning that are attractive, light, clean, safe – and that those engaging spaces exude a sense of calm and purpose sourced in clear expectations of staff about pupils' well-being and attitudes to learning. They are spaces too which are owned and shaped by children.

They are passionate about time being very well used every day, rooted in a curriculum that motivates children and young people to ask deep questions of themselves, take risks in their learning and develop collaborative skills. They are determined that thoughtfully created whole-school systems are applied consistently by all staff; *consistency* is their Holy Grail.

Leaders are joyously obsessive about ensuring that every child is reading at least in line with their actual age, putting in place remedies and extensions to ensure all pupils can access the relevant curriculum. And they try constantly to think and act afresh in relation to those children whose individual special learning needs risk keeping them on the margins.

Critically, top leaders never underestimate that their own unique behaviours set a tone and style for those with whom they work each day. Their emails, for example, are thoughtfully worded, a model to other staff. They shape both the climate and the weather. In the best schools those who lead at all levels are intelligent, optimistic, approachable and in clear, quiet command. Their craft is, if you will, of great simplicity and strength. Their instincts and intuitions are always asking what they can do to make the organisation better.

Restless excellence is about an embedded culture of thinking and doing in which all leaders:

- care more than others think is wise
- risk more than others think is safe
- dream more than others think is practical
- expect more than others think is possible.

Psychologist Anders Ericsson and polemicist Malcolm Gladwell have popularised the idea that 10,000 hours of *purposeful practice* are necessary to create real proficiency, building towards stand-out excellence – whether you are a teacher, a surgeon, a plumber, a Formula One driver or a windsurfer.

There is no doubt that purposeful practice plays a key part in the development of a teacher, but there are teachers new to the profession very capable of delivering excellent lessons; there is sadly a small minority who have practised too long and no longer capture their students' attention. Leaders have a central responsibility to ensure that teachers who are not meeting the required standards are helped to improve rapidly or leave the profession with dignity.

Children get one chance – and the top leaders never forget that.

****

Turning to teachers.

One of the great joys of teaching is that sense of autonomy within your own classroom, free to create a healthy climate for learning and to share your knowledge, skills and expertise with children and young people. Equally, as a teacher you are also part of something bigger than yourself, namely the whole-school community. Good schools are ones where everyone is pulling in the same direction and motivated by the same aspirations – this sense of collaboration infects classrooms and is borne out by the actions and attitudes within them.

A note here about co-teaching, a feature in schools where resources allow. Where two accomplished teachers come together to work with a class for a shorter or longer period, if they have planned their respective roles intelligently the impact on the pupils is significant. Practice in early years and in secondary subjects such as design technology and physical education frequently offer strong models.

If you are in a one-form entry primary school, by definition there is no year team with whom to collaborate, so your team may be by phase or subject. Early years practitioners can be on their own and do not have the daily opportunity to share resources and ideas about exemplary early years practices. Single-teacher departments in secondary schools face the same challenge. So the creation of teams within schools, and linking to colleagues in other schools and settings, becomes very important for teacher well-being and their growth as professionals.

Partnerships of schools, whether formal or informal, are vital to continuous professional development, and it is certainly the case that the very best multi-academy trusts distinguish themselves in the high quality of their investment in staff training.

In special schools there are often as many support staff as teachers, and teams here play a vital role in ensuring that best practices are shared in relation to meeting the learning and therapeutic needs of every child. Too often, special schools can be 'islands', and where they are partnering other special or mainstream schools their teachers value that collaboration and exchange of ideas and resources for what are often complex and demanding classrooms.

In secondary schools, teams come in many forms – academic, curriculum, pastoral – and are pivotal in delivering consistency for students. With teaching plans, assessment, curriculum development, examination preparation, report writing – all of these are delivered successfully by teachers working constructively together.

In all schools, it is collegiality with a personal and professional purpose that matters. Open communication is critical. Teachers of course enjoy the autonomy of their individual classrooms, but they are not islands in the sun. Teachers value the camaraderie of their teams, the support others give them in times of strife, and the opportunity they have in turn to lift the morale of others when most they need it.

One early 20th century writer on schools affirmed that for a teacher 'the perfect combination is sound knowledge, endless patience, and inexhaustible sympathy'. It is rare to find this in one human being, but in teams of good and trusting colleagues there is surely to be found that combination.

ASIDE

Staff Relationship Guidelines – one school's example

Integrity is important. We will achieve this when we do the following:

1. We greet each other.
2. We praise each other and share our successes.
3. We define problems and look for a possible solution – we don't moan.
4. In the face of difficulty we remember that we are part of a team – colleagues are there to support us through good and bad.
5. We are honest – we don't say one thing and think another.
6. We make agreements that we intend and are able to keep.
7. We presume honourable motives – we remember that in the school context, decisions are made in the best interests of our children.
8. We give ourselves time to listen and think.

---

9. In conflict, we talk directly and privately to the person we have a problem with – we don't gossip.

10. We forgive and let go.

Q. What are your thoughts on this list? How do they compare with your school's guidelines?

XCELLENCE

High intention, sincere effort and intelligent execution lie at the epicentre of great schools and great classrooms. So too does a restless excellence. Leaders and teachers are xenacious, even and especially when they are successful in their work. That restlessness to improve never leaves them – and, self-aware, they recognise that same spirit can sometimes unsettle their colleagues.

The epitaph on Sir Christopher Wren's tomb in St Paul's Cathedral reads: 'si monumentum requiris, circumspice' – 'if you seek a monument, look around you'.

Drawing together much of what this A–Z of great classrooms has been exploring, we might conclude that confident teachers in vibrant classrooms can invite any passing visitor to see the cocktail below in action. This is the special double act of teaching and learning, better presented – as the Introduction notes – as an extended Venn diagram.

X features of great classrooms

1. The teacher has *knowledge* effortlessly rising out of them like sap from a tree – and keeps perfecting their craft. Students are inspired.

2. The teacher *commands* the classroom, physically and intellectually, and students respond positively to that expertly planned climate for learning.

3. The *passion* for excellence and scholarship, rooted in the teacher's own achievements, is palpable and often thrilling. Children want to practise, rehearse and emulate top achievements.

4. A teacher's unambiguous set of *values*, embodying integrity and clear conscience, underpin memorable classroom practices. Children feel secure.

5. The *fun* in learning is teachers and students sharing humour and wit, rooted in risk-taking, digression and applying learning beyond the classroom.

6. The *creative* teacher has a predictable unpredictability about their person. Students know they are in for some memorable learning.

7. What teachers *expect* is what they get in any classroom, in any subject, and in any context. Children are no fools; they willingly respond to high expectations.

8. *Empathy* is that vital capacity in a teacher to imagine and understand that the learner may well have a different frame of reference. Students highly respect this.

9. *Resilience* is two-track: one for the pupils' stamina in new learning; and one for the teacher's self-preservation and ultimate flourishing. Both live to teach and learn another day.

10. *Reflecting* on what they are achieving in classrooms becomes the teacher's and the students' habit. Together, they practise being excellent.

ASIDE

A word about independent learning

Y13

Think for a moment about how the schooling system is organised. In the early years we promote experiential learning and purposeful play, indoors and outdoors. As children move up through primary and into secondary, curriculum content dictates a narrowing of opportunities for independent working, no matter how much teachers strive to develop it. Curriculum and examination syllabus coverage trumps all. Then, like a cork out of a champagne bottle, students entering post-16 education are freed again to be more independent learners. The shape of the two paragraphs you are now reading represents a fundamental feature of learning in the institution called school.

Does it have to be this way?

There are increasingly strong arguments that final examinations as we know them today look increasingly anachronistic in a world of people working in teams and employers prizing the three Cs: communication, collaboration, creating. Whilst aspects of the International Baccalaureate treasure those attributes, GCSE and A level manifestly do not. Many in education who are engaged in rethinking assessment rightly contest that, as a starting point, all GCSEs could comprise: 25% oral, 25% final written, 25% portfolio, 25% online. That configuration could come about. And that way, this shape you are reading through can change.

Agreed?

YR

Y = WHY?

Philosophers since ancient times and across cultures have asked the fundamental human questions: what kind of life should we live? Why do we do anything that we do? Each of us will have our own responses to the 'why?' question in terms of what we value in our personal lives. Professionals, in any walk of life, generally answer that their work gives them purpose, fulfilment and an income – they order these words variously. Some answer that it is all about 'vocation', and teaching alongside medicine is a profession where this word frequently surfaces.

The author and leadership expert Simon Sinek's *Start with Why* is about a naturally occurring pattern, a way of thinking, acting and communicating that gives some leaders the ability to inspire those around them. His theory goes that the more organisations and people who learn to start with WHY, the more people there will be who wake up feeling fulfilled by the work they do.

On page 75 the extract from *The Children Act* features a judge faced with a momentous decision as to whether to turn off the life-support machine of a 17-year-old young man. She seeks to sum up what it is to be human, and therefore what she would be depriving the man of. Instructively for this chapter, she mentions 'satisfying work through engagement with demanding tasks', surely a fair description of teaching for those who love its variety, challenges and rewards.

It is the stuff of popular magazines. Interview a famous person about their childhood influences, their treasured moments and possessions, their faith, their biggest extravagance, who and what they find most irritating. One interview asked a Formula One racing driver what his childhood ambition was. He replied: 'To be a farmer – I thought tractors were just brilliant. Then a greenkeeper at a golf course because of all the different lawnmowers. Then I realised you could go a lot faster.'

Another interviewee, a distinguished mathematician, answered the same question with: 'To be a tenpin bowler. Then an astronaut.' And a third admitted: 'To make friends with a wolf.'

One of the standard interview questions invariably elicits thoughtful and illuminating responses: 'Which matters more to success: *ambition* or *talent*?' One person will observe that both are ingredients to success but that luck is even more important. Another will suggest that passion makes the chances of success greater. Yet another will describe a particular teacher they had at school being more important than either ambition or talent. And other keywords arise: opportunity, confidence, inner gift, discipline.

For the Formula One driver above: 'In sport, you've got to have the right body to do what you want to do, but then it's down to hard work.' In the words of one of the UK's leading scientists and vaccine developers: 'So many talented people don't have an idea what they're capable of.'

At the start of every academic year one primary teacher I know displays in her classroom this extract from Miroslav Holub's poem 'A boy's head'.

In it there is a space-ship
And a project
For doing away with piano lessons.
There is a river
That flows upwards.
There is a multiplication table.
There is anti-matter.
And it just cannot be trimmed.
I believe
That only what cannot be trimmed
Is a head.
There is much promise
In the circumstance
That so many people have heads.

It is a reminder to her of the endless possibilities that rest inside the minds of the children who sit in front of her – and that it is her challenge to unlock those possibilities. That is her raison d'être as a teacher.

So what can we all do in our own classrooms to realise the ambitions and talents of those who look to us for guidance and inspiration? To teach a series of lessons is akin to weaving a tapestry: the outline pattern is predetermined, the final outcomes less prescribed and open to the creative process.

Excellent teachers take every opportunity to spot the inner gift of a child. They nurture confidence in the shy student. They help young people to believe in their abilities and develop a latent talent. How a young person feels about themselves – their personal dignity and self-esteem – lies at the heart of a good education.

Excellent teachers everywhere are motivated to teach with invention, rigour and fun. Whether in the early, middle or senior years, teachers relish the unique opportunity they have to take young minds on journeys of discovery. The teacher's optimistic, long-established trade is one of talent-spotting and helping children realise their ambitions – enabling all young people to attain well and achieve with pride. That is why teachers are teachers: there is always much promise in their classrooms. And we are all deeply interested in doing something better tomorrow than we did it today.

I have visited many outstanding schools – that is, schools which, as an inspector applying a particular framework, I have judged to be 'outstanding'. (There are just a few schools in the world which 'stand out' – that is a separate tale.) In the best schools there is a central paradox that runs through them like Brighton through a stick of rock. It is this: the schools are at one and the same time very secure in their values and ways of doing, yet simultaneously restless to improve their practice.

So too with the excellent classroom practitioner, absolutely in the grip of well-tried, tested and effective practices yet simultaneously questing to improve their teaching of a particular topic, concept or skill. Show me the teacher who asks at the end of the day: what have I learned as a teacher today? What shall I do (a) the same and (b) differently next time?

A word on faith education

Many teachers work in faith schools and choose to do so because they believe that a faith-based education provides something distinctive both for them as teachers and for the pupils they teach. Great classrooms in faith schools are underpinned by teachers' explicit modelling of character values and encouraging children to reflect on their place in the world and on the religious mission to which the school belongs.

The words hope, aspiration and courageous advocacy are used by teachers in these classrooms with an emphasis on religious faith. When 'big questions' are posed by teachers across the curriculum, pupils are asked to look beyond themselves, to think globally about life and develop an understanding of disadvantage, deprivation and the exploitation of the natural world from a particular standpoint. (The Statutory Inspection of Anglican and Methodist Schools (SIAMS) Evaluation Framework is worth dipping into by all teachers.)

This is not to say, of course, that social, moral, spiritual and cultural education is the province only of faith schools – far, far from it. But those who teach in faith schools say that their classrooms are enriched by the religious perspective and that, in a sense, this is part of their calling to the profession. Teaching – anywhere, any place – is inherently a moral enterprise.

ASIDE

Why teach? What is schooling all about?

- The aims of education are much wider, and subtler, than the obsession with 'standards', based on a narrow notion of intellectual ability, separate from values.
- Teaching is inherently a moral enterprise.
- Learning is a social process, rooted in relationships and reciprocity, rather than a quest for independence or autonomy.

- Identity is always malleable, so that our intelligence, our abilities and our beliefs are not fixed – but early experience is especially influential in how we relate to other people and regulate our emotional responses.
- Understanding is constructed, not delivered.
- Learning is not entirely, or even primarily, a conscious process.
- Children are not just little adults and childhood not only a preparation for the adult world.
- Unless teachers are motivated, passionate, energetic, engaged and creative – it is unlikely children will be.

Q. Where do you stand on any of the above?

ZOON

... phonanta

As every child is taught, the word alphabet comes from the compound of the two Greek words *alpha* and *beta*. It was the Greeks who called a human being the *zoon phonanta*, meaning literally 'the talking animal'. In the trenchant words of author Anthony Burgess: 'What makes humanity different from the brute creation is its capacity for constructing a system of auditory signs which stand not only for its thoughts and feelings about the outside world but for the outside world itself'.

I began my working life in education in HM Prison Brixton, in the days of slopping out. Lingering smells, jangling keys and turbulent landings I recall to this day. All educators should spend time in the education department of one of His Majesty's prisons. It is a poignant reminder that basic literacy is a birthright that should be denied nobody. My teaching commitment of adult literacy was to small groups of young men who had put a proverbial bottle through someone's face on a Saturday night when they found themselves unable to articulate their way out of a confrontation.

When I then moved into full-time teaching in south London primary and secondary schools, I vowed that no child I taught would end up in prison and that the greatest gift for life that I could afford them was confidence with spoken and written language.

In my later days at the National Literacy Trust establishing the 'Reading Is *Fun*damental' charity, I used to give talks entitled 'Have you ever met a mugger who's read *Middlemarch*?' This was my way of saying that whatever else we do for children and young people in classrooms, we must give them the dignity of being able to speak, read and write with fluency to make their way in the endlessly fascinating global society which they inhabit. Confident literacy and oracy are a fundamental matter of self-esteem and personal dignity.

So it is the teaching and learning of language in all its rich complexity that must underpin all classrooms, pretty much wherever they are on the planet and whatever the local language – and that is equally true in an early years setting or in an IB Biology seminar.

The poet T.S. Eliot in *Four Quartets* testifies that success in language is a partial business, 'a new beginning, a raid on the inarticulate', at best a muddled string of attempts to define and redefine the nature of one's being, to rationalise its presence in society.

George Steiner, one of the outstanding linguists of the twentieth century, wrote exhaustively on the global challenges of language in which those of English are but a significant enclave. Why four thousand or more languages he asks? Why, by a factor of a thousand, more languages than human blood types? Every people has some variant on the Tower of Babel in its mythology. There exists a proliferation of neighbouring tongues that has been one of the most intractable barriers to human collaboration and economic progress. Arguably, in a digital and mobile phone age, we speak more to say less; we hear more and listen less.

This is the global context within which the English language is taught and learnt in our schools.

Of all language activities, writing is the most artificial and the one with which most of us struggle from time to time. No wonder then that many children should find writing problematic and that they are surrounded with assumptions and popular shibboleths about how it can be taught and improved.

Writing imposes demands on the performer which do not characterise in the same way either our other active use of language (talking) or our receptive ones (reading and listening). And just as we cannot wholly know or evidence what we are going to say on paper until we have written it, so it is with speech – our recognitions and perceptions are less articulate, less explicit before they are shared.

Language in action comprises vocabulary, phonology, grammar, tone, emphases.

We can alter our meaning by being polite, aggressive or tentative and by modifying tonal quality, timing, stress and juncture. Speech is a process of censoring, changing in midstream, restarting, irrelevant interruption, hesitancy and delaying monosyllabic utterances. Speech and language are a complicated business we probably take for granted. 'It just comes naturally', the saying goes. But for millions of children in our schools, speech and language do not flow naturally at all.

From its extensive research, the national charity Speech and Language UK estimates that approaching 1.7 million children and young people have obstacles to fluency, obstacles that through their school years damage self-esteem and certainly hinder academic progress. My own research in chairing the Association of School and College Leaders (ASCL)'s commission *The Forgotten Third* (2019) identified fractured literacy and oracy at the heart of many students' academic and examination difficulties.

It is a sad reflection on the English schooling system that if the national inspectorate plays a certain tune, then all schools dance to that tune. Ofsted's current focus on reading is testimony to that – and that is proving no bad thing. But before reading and writing, there is speech and language – and as a school system we need to get much better at developing all pupils' skills in this arena.

This begins with families at home and is then a vibrant and vital continuum from ages 3 to 18. An ambitious raid on the inarticulate needs to underpin every primary, special and secondary classroom, every day. Our children and young people deserve nothing less if they are to enter society as confident, conversational human beings.

****

In all schools, then, there need to be two key goals in what we might call a whole-school language collaborative:

- For students: the dignity and positive self-esteem of being able to speak, read and write with fluency – thereby impacting on attainment and achievement across the curriculum

- For teachers: the central importance of 'every teacher is a teacher of the English language', making that explicit in daily practice in all classrooms.

These key goals need to be underpinned by a consistent and innovative focus on:

1. Enhancing *students' literacy* in the context of their cultural capital: 'the best that has been thought and said'. We want our children and young people to be effective readers and writers, leading to attainment without a whiff of glass ceilings.

2. Improving pupils' command of *academic language*: knowing their way around textbooks and resources, and being able to apply new vocabulary in their well-presented and fluent writing.

3. Placing an explicit emphasis – within and beyond classrooms – on pupils' high quality *oracy and articulacy*: e.g. answering orally in full sentences with clear articulation; presenting TED Talks to embed knowledge and understanding.

At the beating heart of great primary, special and secondary classrooms, the fun and fundamentals of language should underpin all lessons. We want *children* to relish the words they are using. And, irrespective of topic or subject, we want *teachers*, in the words of the Teachers' Standards, 'to demonstrate an understanding of and take responsibility for promoting high standards of literacy'.

ASIDE

Making language explicit in our classrooms

1. Using a glossary as a talk tool

Students keep a glossary at the back of their books, noting command vocabulary and 'advanced language' in and around their subject of study. Teachers encourage pupils to have the glossary open on their desks and to use the advanced language in their oral responses in lessons. The glossary becomes a living language document, not just a list of words.

2. What's special about your subject?

Ask students to listen extra carefully in one of your lessons and note down ten words that are subject specific. For homework, ask them to look up the meaning and etymology of the words. In class, have a discussion about whether the words *are* subject specific, or actually occur in other subjects too. Help students make connections between subjects across the curriculum. As a starter, try the word 'differentiation' as it applies in mathematics and biology!

3. What's common across languages?

Ask students who are studying/speaking more than one language to make a note in their books of vocabulary that shares common roots. Could they give a five-minute TED Talk or produce some classroom posters on their findings? How can they embed that vocabulary to help them remember it, especially for tests and examinations?

4. What assessment language used by the teacher is helpful?

Ask students to share their thoughts on the language the teacher uses when she or he is engaged in formative and summative assessment, orally and in writing/marking. Do teachers use a shared language, or different words and phrases? Discuss with students how their 'next best steps' are most usefully supported by a teacher's particular use of language/vocabulary.

5. Examination papers

Give out a set of national test or examination papers. Ask students to highlight any words which they feel uncertain about, focusing on how a word is being used in the examination question. Ask them to write down the word and a dictionary definition. Share it and discuss with a partner. The teacher can draw this together and highlight the 'must-understand' jargon of a test paper.

Q. What techniques and activities on language would you add here which you know work well in classrooms? What do your students say about learning vocabulary which would help them most with their tests and examinations?

READING 7

Marsha Ivins, a veteran of five space shuttle missions who logged over 1,300 hours in space, was asked by one of our students, 'So how do you go to toilet in space?' Her smile told me it was a question she had often fielded. Her answer, although given hundreds of times by her, was original for every child asking the question for the first time.

It was a prelude to a real conversation about living in space in which she made science real for all of us. Why? Because our kids wanted to know.

Today, the influence and impact that visitors can have in our classrooms has been expanded through access to technology. Without ever leaving the confines of our own rooms we can talk to a climber at the base camp of Everest, to a surgeon preparing for a complex brain surgery, interview a footballer straight from her team's success in the World Cup, or simply sit with a grandparent reflecting on her life in the comfort of her own home with a cup of chai in her hands.

Of all the things I have learned as an educator over the years is something I have always really known as a teacher. The most profound and yet simple revelation is that students learn best when they are involved in their own learning with each other undertaking real activities.

They won't always be as breathtaking as standing with a climber on the roof of the world talking about the impact of altitude on the human body. Sometimes they will be as simple as primary children listening to and asking questions of local trades people as part of their unit of enquiry. When our students are watching a chai walah prepare the tea for his customers, working with an artist as she helps us create colours, or learning with a writer how to craft the words to create our own pictures – *all* are engaged.

What is truly surprising is how few of us see our classrooms as windows onto the world. Fortunately, especially now as we emerge from the global pandemic, more teachers and schools are looking for ways to enrich student learning by expanding their horizons.

It doesn't matter where our schools are or what curriculum we follow. All we need to do is to find out the work and passions of our parents and local community and then match these against our curriculum. Bringing people into school, sending our children out from school, whether physically or virtually, is in all of our grasps.

Why not open your classroom window even more widely to let the world in?

Malcolm Wheeler

SECTION
TWO

SPECIAL EDUCATIONAL NEEDS: GREAT CLASSROOMS

The same themes and trails of the A–Z approach follow below, refocused on special schools and children and young people with special educational needs in mainstream classrooms. This can serve as a celebration of best practices and as a checklist for self-evaluation.

1. The journey to the classroom is a positive experience

- There is a collective responsibility for the wider school environment, with pupils and staff sharing that responsibility. Everyone ensures that the whole-school behaviour policy is applied at all times in all locations.
- The journey is used to develop skills – e.g. independence. Are all the pupils who could come in by themselves enabled to do so?
- Staff and pupils greet one another using developmentally appropriate approaches, creating a warm and welcoming environment conducive to effective learning.

2. Warm relationships, humour and clear expectations shape the classroom ethos and values; students value one another's contributions

- Staff are measured and consistent in their responses, and build relationships which promote success and which visibly celebrate the contributions of all pupils, irrespective of need.
- Language is used skilfully to enable expectations to be understood at all times – particularly when working with children exhibiting emotional distress.
- The significance of an achievement or contribution is often defined by the individual child and celebrated as such.

3. Teachers/lecturers know and enthuse about their subject, and know their students as individuals

- Staff recognise the risks of generalisations based on social, medical or psychological labels.
- Every child is treated as a unique individual and their education is bespoke to them, informed by careful assessment to identify their developmental priorities.
- Staff fill the resourcing gaps within their subjects, both physically and intellectually. They maximise the school's knowledge base by developing resources, curricula and assessments rather than purchasing those of others.

4. The classroom walls and ceiling promote the subject and students' high quality work.

- Careful consideration is given to appropriate visual and tactile displays, and their positioning in classrooms and common spaces.
- Displays reflect the full range of communicative need within the school – work produced by the pupils is accessible to the pupils.
- All types of achievement are reflected in the displays, even those which leave no permanent outcome. Video, photo, audio, tablets are harnessed creatively.

5. Well-prepared resources mean that teaching and learning flow.

- Resources are carefully matched to the agreed curriculum framework and to the needs of the child, and where not available are developed within the school.
- 'Pedagogical Magpies': the school takes the best of many resources/ approaches, combining them to create that which suits the learning objectives, ethos, pupils' needs.
- Collaboration between staff in developing resources is a hallmark; they review the impact of those resources regularly and adapt them accordingly.

6. Time is skilfully orchestrated; everyone shares the story of the lesson.

- Pace is seen as a tool for maximising impact on learning and is informed by a deep understanding of the pupils' individual needs.
- Knowing when to *pause* and *stop* is just as important as knowing when to start.
- Lesson formats and durations are determined by individual need and what best suits the promotion of success – e.g. 1:1 short bursts; sustained group work; community-based work for a half day.

7. 'Learning prompts' enhance the learning experience of the classroom/laboratory, etc.

- A communicatively rich environment is created in which learning prompts are integrated into the wider school.
- Pupils are not perceived or defined as being a 'type' of communicator, recognising that while they may have a primary communication tool, they may also benefit from access to a wide range of tools at different times and for different purposes.
- Layers of supporting information are provided to help pupils secure understanding in different subjects: symbol-based keywords, signing, formal and informal objects of reference.

8. Individual, pair, group and whole-class activities serve a purpose.

- Opportunities are taken to use different learning structures for the generalisation of knowledge. Is what is learned 1:1 applicable in a group, outside the classroom, at different times, with different resources?
- Groupings are diverse, promoting an inclusive culture, supported by highly effective differentiation.
- Learning is meaningful and transferable beyond the school day and ultimately beyond formal education.

9. Students are practised in independent study skills, and self- and peer-review.

- Explicit and creative opportunities are created to enable pupils to work independently.
- Pupils are enabled to value one another's work and recognise that success is relative. One pupil may be rewarded for sitting calmly while another may have to complete a page of writing.
- Pupils draw attention sensitively to the successes of their peers.

10. Homework is fit for purpose: academic and applied learning are in balance.

- Homework, rooted in the planned curriculum, is set with the intention of pupils sharing with their families what they have achieved in school.
- Activities are set to encourage pupils to practise at home a new skill they have learned at school.
- The emphasis is on learning at school being transferable to home and other environments.

11. Systems of marking and assessment track students' progress and show them how to move forward.

- Assessment is used to inform understanding of a pupil's development, enabling teachers to identify the best next step on an *individualised* basis.
- Assessments are developed by staff to fill the gaps left by the commercially available assessment tools: 'small steps' must be recognised and shared with students and parents.
- Teachers and other adults take a systematic approach to assessment and revisit previous assessments regularly to ensure knowledge has been securely acquired by pupils.

12. Skilful, probing questioning permeates: 'surprise' and 'scholarship' feature.

- There is a keen awareness of how a pupil's comprehension and expression skills can fluctuate, and what factors can influence this.

- Language use is differentiated to support individual ability levels.
- Scaled language approaches are used to enable pupils to successfully comprehend, supported with additional communicative tools where appropriate.

13. Music, video, internet clips bring laughter and diversion.

- The potential of various media for summarising learning and for sharing outcomes with pupils and parents is well harnessed.
- The use of video to capture transient moments of success and joy, building portfolios of evidence, is routine.
- A multi-sensory environment is creatively and imaginatively developed; it is sensitive and not overwhelming.

14. Digression is treasured; praise is given when earned.

- Praise and reward are used as sophisticated tools to shape positive behaviours, avoiding simplistic cause and effect interactions.
- Staff are well aware that pupils' reactions to praise and reward may be diverse, and these are managed consciously and intelligently. A child who finds being the centre of attention challenging may prefer a casual comment while social confidence is built.
- The learning that is happening is not always that which is planned, but is just as valuable – it is recognised when a shift in focus can be used to everyone's advantage.

15. Evaluation of sessions by students is valued and acted upon.

- Staff interpret the behaviours and attitudes to learning within specific lessons, making pupils aware of their levels of engagement and communication.
- Pupils are given a vocabulary for self-review, including how they feel about *what* they are learning and *how* they are making progress.
- Evaluation does not need to be explicit or permanently captured, but it is important to value all pupils' capacity to contribute if verbal and written feedback are not accessible to all.

16. Coda: for whole-school reflections on educating pupils with special educational needs in any setting.

- How are all staff enabled to actively promote learning – site staff, therapists, medical staff, midday carers, administrative team?
- How is learning taken into real-life situations? How do you know that what your pupils learn has a meaningful impact on their wider life?
- What is the school's role in the wider community and how does it promote the abilities of pupils to function successfully beyond the school gates?
- What do your pupils achieve once they have left school and how does this inform classroom practice?
- Striking the balance between consistency and uniformity: how do we ensure there are clear messages and a strong collective ethos without stifling individuality and innovation in the classroom?
- How do you decide what *not* to do in your school? 'Bandwagons we haven't jumped on.'

****

Less Able

He could not describe the beauty that surrounded him:
The soft green dale and craggy hills.
He could not spell the names
Of those mysterious places which he knew so well.
But he could snare a rabbit, ride a horse,
Repair a fence and dig a dyke,
Drive a tractor, plough a field,
Milk a cow and lamb a ewe,
Name a bird by a faded feather
Smell the seasons and predict the weather,
That less able child could.
Gervase Phinn

BLINKS: DO YOU SEE WHAT I SEE?

Year 6 Lesson Blink

1. What are your first impressions of the learning environment?

- Is it light, airy and the right temperature for learning?
- Does the classroom, and do the areas around it, reflect the range of upper primary work? What is special, or striking, about this work?
- Is the classroom arranged so that all children can be involved in discussions and also use their workspace to write, design and implement?
- How do the children react to your presence as a visitor? Are they happy to talk and explain?

2. In what ways does the style of teaching and learning reflect that this is a Year 6 class and therefore distinctive in terms of the completion of the primary stage of learning?

3. How is furniture configured? Where does the teacher position her/himself?

4. To what extent do the children take control of their learning and how able are they to explore a range of learning areas? Are the children aware of what will come next in terms of their move to the secondary phase?

5. How are support staff being deployed to have a significant impact on learning?

6. What evidence can you see of Year 6's independent learning skills? If the teacher left the room, would the children continue to work on the current task?

7. Is the level of work appropriate for the more able learners and is it sufficiently demanding? Has the work been effectively scaffolded, whilst retaining an intrinsic interest/challenge, for those who have learning or personal management difficulties?

8. Is homework or other independent study/research important to the lesson? Has there been some form of lead-in and are there possibilities for extension?

9. How well does the teacher demonstrate his/her own specialist subject knowledge? Does she or he extend horizons and leave students magically wondering?

10. How creatively are book/technology resources harnessed to stimulate students' interest and extend their skills and knowledge?

****

Year 12 Lesson Blink

1. What are your first impressions of the learning environment?

- Does the room celebrate the specialist subject being taught?
- Does the room celebrate post-16 work?

2. In what ways does the style of teaching and learning reflect that this is a Year 12 class and not a Year 8 class?

3. In the time you are in the room, count the minutes (a) the teacher talks (b) students converse with a proper focus. Is the teacher working harder than the students?

4. What evidence can you see of Year 12's independent learning skills? If the teacher left the room, would students' focus continue? Do the students teach each other?

5. Is the level of work appropriate for more able students, irrespective of mixed-ability or setted group? If not, how would you make it more demanding?

6. How has homework led into this lesson? How is homework/further independent study/research following up the lesson?

7. What evidence is there of (a) fun (b) scholarship (c) intriguing digressions (d) teacher sharing personal enthusiasms (e) students' intellectual confidence?

8. How well does the teacher demonstrate his or her own specialist subject knowledge? Does she or he extend horizons and leave students magically wondering?

9. How creatively are book/technology resources harnessed to stimulate students' interest and extend their skills and knowledge?

10. Can you tell from looking at books/folders/online files whether students fully understand syllabus demands ('the story of their learning')? Is there a difference in the quality of note-taking amongst students? Is 'next best step' marking well judged?

DICTATION

A. What's the point?

One of the most effective teaching tools is dictation. It is widely used across the curriculum in different countries, but is significantly underused in schools in the UK, often deemed to belong to an era of rote learning. Some primary and secondary teachers harness its full potential, mainly in literacy, English and Modern Foreign Languages (MFL) lessons – but its power lies right across the curriculum to embed knowledge and understanding.

Dictation provides simultaneous practice in listening, reading, writing, memory recall and proofreading. Done regularly, dictation is transformational in building stamina in writing.

B. How to lead it

1. Outline the purpose and the process of the dictation, as set out above and below.

2. Choose a fiction or non-fiction piece of text, one you may be using in class linked to the science, geography or art curriculum. It could be the memorable openings of a great novel, speech, world-renowned text – something to give relevance, to enhance cultural capital, to make the reader sit up!

3. Try this one, words taken from the American Declaration of Independence (1776):

> We hold these truths to be self-evident, that all men are created equal, that they are endowed by their creator with certain unalienable rights, that among these are life, liberty and the pursuit of happiness. That to secure these rights, governments are instituted among men, deriving their just powers from the consent of the governed. That whenever any form of government becomes destructive of these ends, it is the right of the people to

alter or to abolish it, and to institute new government, laying its foundations on such principles and organising its powers in such form, as to them shall seem most likely to effect their safety and happiness. Prudence indeed will dictate that governments long established should not be changed for light and transient causes.

4. Give every pupil their own copy of the text.

5. Read aloud the passage twice, all eyes on the text. Ask a pupil to read it a third time.

6. Ask the pupils to please put away the text so they cannot see it.

7. Begin reading the passage in short phrases, repeating each phrase not more than once; pupils start writing what they hear in their best handwriting. They concentrate on their writing only, no distractions or questions. They keep up with your reading as best they can. If they miss something, tell them not to worry and to move on with you.

8. Read the whole passage in this way, phrase by phrase, indicating where punctuation marks appear. With practice, pupils will not need to know this.

9. Pause and say: 'That's the end for now. I am going to read the whole passage one last time. I want you to follow carefully and make any corrections you think are necessary so that you have written every word accurately. You look only at your own writing, no one else's.'

10. Reread the passage clearly and at a pace you judge is suitable for your class.

11. Now ask pupils to swap their own writing with someone who is not sitting next to them – this is important.

12. Then ask pupils to turn back to the original text and, slowly and carefully, proofread and correct legibly (different colour) the pupil's writing in front of them. You can add on a fun numerical mark scheme and prizes of pens or similar as you judge for your class.

13. Once marked, pupils hand back the work to its originator. You give time for everyone to check over what they got right and what errors they made. Discuss these as you judge. Everyone then rewrites the whole

passage, with determined accuracy in their best writing.

14. Then the passage is read out a final time by a couple of different pupil voices.

15. Complete. File carefully so that pupils can see how their dictation work improves over time.

The whole process, once embedded – 30 minutes. Not a moment wasted.

EXAMPLES FROM SCHOOLS

1. THE PEDAGOGICAL RUBRIC

ST CHRISTOPHER'S

Pedagogical Rubric

Lesson or partial **lesson observations** by a HoD/YL/SLT member(s), who will be looking for aspects of excellent practice as described in the **Pedagogical Rubric**. It is expected that not all elements from the Pedagogical Rubric are met within a single lesson observation. However, over a period of time, it is expected that all elements are met. There are four possible categories for the individual descriptors within the Pedagogical Rubric:

- Instructor - the teacher has mastered this element of the rubric and is able to conduct CPD in this area and support colleagues;

- Confident - the teacher is confident in their own practice of this element but further consolidation is required before they conduct CPD and support colleagues;
- Not observed - this element has not yet been observed or demonstrated by the teacher;
- Not yet met - the teacher has tried to demonstrate this element but has not yet met the Confident descriptor.

REVIEWING MATERIAL	
Confident	**Instructor**
The teacher begins most lessons with a short review of previous learning (including homework where appropriate). Clear links are made between new and previous learning. Students are given opportunities to overlearn new skills, knowledge and concepts.	The teacher is especially adept at identifying the skills, knowledge and concepts and instilling the attitude that students will need to master. Careful planning of the consolidation of new skills and concepts is evident in all lessons.
Within and across units, the teacher provides frequent opportunities through formal and informal assessments for students to review previous learning.	The teacher has established a structured system of review in which students regularly consolidate previous learning and apply it in new and unfamiliar contexts.
Reflections and goals	

QUESTIONING AND CONSOLIDATING/CHECKING FOR UNDERSTANDING	
Confident	**Instructor**
The teacher asks a variety of open and closed questions which are differentiated in most cases. Students are expected to explain, clarify or justify their responses with appropriate levels of sophistication.	The teacher's questioning strategies are very well developed, both in terms of the range of techniques used and their impact on the students' learning.
The teacher regularly checks the students' understanding of instructions and concepts, and students' responses often inform the pace and course of a lesson.	The teacher involves all students when clarifying or extending their understanding, and students' responses consistently inform the pace and course of lessons.
Strategies such as wait time and 'no hands up' are used effectively. The majority of students are actively engaged in dialogue with the teacher.	Insightful questioning and effective strategies are used consistently to check students' understanding of instructions and concepts.
The teacher's questions often focus on the learning skills being developed in lessons.	The teacher actively defines and facilitates metacognitive processes through questioning strategies, design of tasks and student interactions.
Reflections and goals	

SEQUENCING CONCEPTS AND MODELLING	
Confident	**Instructor**
Lessons are well structured and planned, with each step in the students' learning clearly identified. Time is given to consolidate specific skills/concepts before the next is introduced.	The teacher is especially adept at managing the steps in each student's learning. Mini-plenaries are regularly used to consolidate the students' understanding and identify misconceptions.
The teacher regularly models approaches to tasks, noting each of the steps involved in completing them.	Worked examples are particularly well planned and modelled, with the teacher clearly identifying the principles behind each step in the process.
The teacher makes effective use of mark schemes, rubrics and concrete materials to scaffold the students' understanding of new concepts. The teacher anticipates and pre-empts likely errors or misconceptions.	The teacher's choice of scaffolds is especially well chosen and these are adapted to suit the needs of the different students in the class. Student errors are regularly used as learning opportunities.
Lessons are clearly differentiated and challenge is evident at all ability levels. Instances of a mis-match between tasks set and a students' ability are quickly identified and rectified.	Differentiation of tasks indicates both an excellent subject knowledge and an astute judgement of the students' individual learning needs.

Reflections and goals

STAGES OF PRACTICE	
Confident	**Instructor**
The teacher allows sufficient time to introduce new concepts, asking questions to check for understanding and closely supervising students as they practise new skills.	The teacher uses a variety of strategies to enable students to assimilate new material. Students' are very well prepared for independent practice and minimal independent learning time is lost through misconceptions.
Lessons are well planned with different levels of challenge to ensure that most students are secure with each step in their learning before moving on to the next.	Lessons contain a personalised level of challenge for groups of students or individual students as required, with a clear emphasis on the thorough mastery of skills and concepts.
Students are provided with ample opportunities to consolidate new skills, knowledge and concepts through class and home learning.	Lessons are well structured to ensure skills, knowledge and concepts are thoroughly understood and connections are made by students with prior learning.

Reflections and goals

LEARNING ENVIRONMENT	
Confident	**Instructor**
The learning environment is organised in such a way as to maximise teaching time. Resources are readily available to students and displays support the students' learning. Shared learning materials are of a high quality.	The arrangement of the learning environment and its resources is particularly efficient and effective. Displays are highly stimulating and support students' learning. Practical and electronic materials shared with the students are of a the highest quality.

Reflections and goals

STUDENTS' RESPONSE	
Confident	**Instructor**
Students are engaged with their learning and are on task for most of the lesson. They are able to work with a good degree of independence and concentration appropriate to their age. Many students demonstrate a positive mindset when approaching tasks.	Students are exceptionally focused and enthusiastic. They demonstrate positivity and resourcefulness when undertaking tasks, and will independently reflect on their learning. Students of all abilities consistently show a positive mindset.
Students are encouraged to ask questions in the course of lessons and they are able to articulate these clearly.	The students' questioning skills are very well developed and they ask thoughtful, precise questions to clarify and extend their understanding. The teacher provides frequent opportunities for students to develop and refine these skills.

Reflections and goals

RELATIONSHIPS	
Confident	**Instructor**
A good rapport between students and the teacher is evident. Interactions are warm, honest and purposeful. The teacher clearly recognises the differing needs of the students and demonstrates empathy for them. Any behavioural issues are low level and dealt with consistently by the teacher.	Relationships between students and with the teacher are exceptionally positive and mutually respectful. The students are clearly motivated by the teacher's enthusiastic and engaging manner. Low level behaviour incidents are rare.

Reflections and goals

2. CONCISE LESSON OBSERVATION   ST CHRISTOPHER'S

Concise Lesson Observation
The criteria are key extracts from the Pedagogical Rubric

Name of staff:		Subject:
Year group:		Period:
Criteria		**Comments and feedback**
1. The teacher reviews and consolidates learning effectively	• How effectively does the teacher review and consolidate previous learning? • If observed, how is informal or formal assessment used to review and retrieve learning? • Is time given to review and consolidate learning before moving on to new learning, e.g. using mini-plenaries?	
2. The teacher regularly checks for understanding	• Does the teacher make regular checks of students' understanding to inform the pace and course of the lesson? • Does the teacher use strategies (e.g. no hands up) and questioning effectively to check for understanding? • How effectively does the teacher help students to check, monitor and evaluate their own learning?	

3. Stages of practice build students' knowledge and allow them to apply their knowledge as skills	• Do new knowledge and skills build on what has been taught before? • How well are students prepared for independent practice? • How does the teacher make use of formative assessment and retrieval practice to help students build and apply knowledge? • Is the lesson planned and structured so that knowledge and skills are thoroughly learnt and practised?	
4. Learning is differentiated and challenging	• Does the teacher have high expectations for student learning and outcomes? • Do all students in the lesson make expected progress? • Are lessons suitably differentiated to allow for appropriate challenge for all students? • If observed, are scaffolds well chosen and adapted to support different students' learning? • If observed, how well planned and effective is the teacher's use of worked examples and modelling in supporting students' learning?	
5. Teacher communication and presentation are clear, engaging and enthusiastic	• Does the teacher communicate subject knowledge clearly and effectively? • Is the lesson well paced? • Does the teacher have an enthusiasm and engagement that motivates learners? • Are resources clear, accessible and presented in a manner that reduces cognitive load?	

6. The learning environment	• Is the learning environment efficient and effective? • Are displays highly stimulating and do they support students' learning?	
7. The teacher has established supportive, positive relationships. Student behaviour is focused on learning	• Does the teacher show empathy for and understanding of their students? • Is there evidence of mutual respect and a positive rapport? • Do students ask thoughtful and insightful questions about their learning? • Are students focused on learning and enthusiastic? • What evidence is there of students' positive mindset?	

Developmental feedback

3. SEVEN PRINCIPLES OF EFFECTIVE REVISION
WEST LONDON FREE SCHOOL

7 Principles of Effective Revision

Effective revision is key to academic success. However, you have to know how to revise. Follow these seven principles, and they will set you on the road to success.

1. **Make a long-term plan**: All of the revision you have to do can seem intimidating, so stop worrying, and start planning. Create a day-by-day plan scheduling exactly what you want to revise when and stick to it.

2. *Do not* **just re-read information**: The least effective type of revision is re-reading notes. Highlighting notes is no better. Both approaches are too passive. You need to be doing something active with your brain to ensure that the information sticks.

3. **Quiz yourself**: For 'finger-tip' knowledge such as historical dates, Spanish verb endings, or chemical formulae, you need to practise recalling information from memory using quizzes. How? flashcards, phone apps, and knowledge organisers.

4. **Stay mentally active**: If you are thinking hard, you are revising well. Therefore, devise tasks that allow you to practise the thinking you have to do in the real exam. How? Write plans for practice questions, create mind maps, and complete past papers.

5. **Create memory aids**: For that really difficult information that just won't stick, create a memory aid. This can be a silly joke, a mnemonic, or a visual representation. Find out what works for you, and use it.

6. **Focus on the hard stuff**: It is tempting to revise topics you already know, as it feels nice and reassuring. However, this is 'comfort blanket' revision. Put away the comfort blanket and focus on the topics you find difficult. That is where the biggest gains are made.

7. **Work hard, then have a break**: Either be revising, or on a break. Put your phone away, turn off your music, and close that internet browser. Then, when you have completed your revision, you can have fun. But don't try to mix the two.

4. SEVEN PRINCIPLES OF PUBLIC SPEAKING WEST LONDON FREE SCHOOL

7 Principles of Public Speaking at West London Free School

1. **Understand the text**: Fully understand the meaning of the text, whether you have written it or not. Go through it carefully beforehand, and ask if you need help. Once you do understand the meaning of the text, underline words you should emphasise, and put dashes in the text where you should pause.

2. **Project your voice**: Your words need to be heard clearly throughout the room. Try to visualise your voice hitting the back wall of the room you're speaking in, and speak slightly more loudly than you think you need to.

3. **Control your pace**: Don't speak too quickly, yet still speak with energy and manipulate the pace at which you speak to add greater emphasis to your words. Take a deep breath before you start to speak, and consciously try to pause at the end of each sentence; plan where you might want to speed up or slow down.

4. **Articulate each word**: Make sure that each individual word can be clearly heard and distinguished from those around it. Practise reading your speech aloud, and focus in particular on any words you find difficult to pronounce; type a word into Google to hear it being pronounced or ask someone to help you.

5. **Maintain a good posture**: Stand straight with your shoulders back and feet shoulder-width apart, giving the impression of confidence to the audience. You might want to practise your posture in front of a mirror; when you do get up to speak, take a moment to check your posture before you actually start speaking.

6. **Make eye contact**: Look up and make eye contact with the audience while you are talking. Practise your speech really well beforehand, so that you aren't too reliant on your notes and can have the confidence to look up at the audience.

7. **Keep going**: Keep going even after stumbling over a word and take it in your stride. Remember that everyone slips up when speaking in public — it's completely normal! — so don't worry about any stumbles and just force yourself to keep going.

5. ROUTINES AND HABITS   GARTH HILL COLLEGE

 WHY? To create a calm, purposeful environment that enables pupils and staff to maximise learning time and feel safe and secure at school.

LINE UP	Pupils must:	Teachers will:	Common Language:
This will promote a calm and purposeful atmosphere at the start of the day and lessons.	• Remove coats, scarves, phones, devices and headphones before entering block • Line up silently, single file, facing forward, outside the classroom • Greet tutor/teacher and enter room • Stand behind chair in silence.	• Greet pupils at door • Ensure pupils follow routine • Check uniform • **No exceptions – repeat as needed.**	*Line up in silence* *Face forward* *Ready to learn.*
ROLL CALL	Pupils must:	Teachers will:	Common Language:
This will ensure pupils are prepared for their learning and teachers can begin the lessons without delay or conflict.	• Greet tutor at the door and enter in silence • Stand in silence behind chair • Ensure TFL are placed on desk • Answer 'Yes Miss/Sir' to the register (in lessons too) • Hold up TFL for checking • Remain silent during checks • Sit down in seating plan once signal is given.	• Meet and greet • Ensure pupils are silent; TFL on desk • Call out TFL and check one by one • Record missing TFL, issue replacement • On completion, signal to leader, wait for 'sign off' to sit • Complete register • Follow tutor schedule.	*Ready to learn.*

TRANSITION	Pupils must:	Teachers will:	Common Language:

This will maintain a calm and orderly environment within and outside the school building.	• Keep to the left
	• Walk forward, sensibly, quietly
	  • Max. two side by side in corridors/walkways
	  • single file on the stairs
	• Keep moving, but wait patiently if busy
	• No phones, devices, headphones visible in blocks, stairwells or walkways
	• Hold the door for others.
		• Issue uniform detentions and/or confiscate devices as appropriate.	*Calm and orderly*
			
			Keep to the left-hand side
			
			No phones, devices, headphones
			
			We are a non-contact school.

LESSON START	Pupils must:	Teachers will:	Common Language:
This routine will ensure purposeful learning.	• Enter in silence and stand behind chair • Place TFL on desk, coats/bags under the table • Sit down when given permission, sit up and forward • Follow hand signal, hands on desk, eyes on teacher, no talking! • Classroom Managers carry out their tasks • Write title, date, WALT (DUMTUMS) • Raise hand to question/speak — no calling out.	• Plan a starter activity for every lesson • Take register as pupils complete starter activity • Ensure pupils sit as per seating plan and stay on task • NB: pupils should sit up and forward unless activity warrants turning around • Indicate a GO Green activity • NB: Only water is permitted in class (not in labs).	*Ready to learn* *5,4,3,2,1 (with hand signal)* *One voice all ears* *No calling out.*

LESSON END	Pupils must:	Teachers will:	Common Language:
This routine will ensure a calm finish to lessons.	• Wait for teacher to indicate the end of lesson • Stand behind chair in silence • Wait to be dismissed.	• Indicate to pupils when it is time to pack up • Ensure pupils are standing silently behind their chairs • Staggered dismissal (eg. row by row, table by table).	*Ready to leave.*

6. LEARNING COMPETENCIES INTERNATIONAL SCHOOL OF GENEVA

Learning competencies

Lifelong learning: knowing how to learn affords people the regenerative capacity to reinvent themselves for changing contextual demands. It is the source of currency, innovation, adaptability, agility and resilience.

Self-agency: this demands capacity and empowerment to analyse the demands of one's environment and apply all resources at hand (knowledge, skills, technologies) to take self-benefiting and self-fulfilling action.

Interactively using diverse tools and resources: these tools include intellectual, cultural, religious, linguistic, material, technical, fiscal, physical and virtual resources, the interface of the self and machines in smart factories as envisaged in the concept Industry 4.0, the use of multiple technologies, and of time.

Interacting with others: this demands collaboration to resolve complex problems and create integrated solutions across contexts. It reaches beyond productivity to humanity. It is also a key competence for social interaction, social cohesion, harmony, justice, and ultimately a peaceful and reconciled future.

Interacting with the world: this enables awareness, sensitivity, and advocacy for collective challenges and opportunities at a local, national, regional and global level.

It entails multi-cultural, multi-religious, multi-lingual perspectives that embrace diversity as an enriching asset.

Multi-literateness: the 21st century requires people to be multi-literate and to deploy these literacies flexibly. These go beyond reading, writing and arithmetic to include micro competencies like digital, cultural, financial, health and media literacies.

Trans-disciplinarity: increasing complexity requires ever more sophisticated solutions that integrate knowledge from multiple disciplines and from domains of knowledge.

TEACHERS' STANDARDS

The Teachers' Standards, first published in 2011 as Crown Copyright material, have stood the test of time in classrooms in England. They have been sourced by many other countries in developing their own standards for classroom teaching. The Standards are reproduced here for cross-reference with the A–Z listings.

PREAMBLE

Teachers make the education of their pupils their first concern, and are accountable for achieving the highest possible standards in work and conduct. Teachers act with honesty and integrity; have strong subject knowledge, keep their knowledge and skills as teachers up-to-date and are self-critical; forge positive professional relationships; and work with parents in the best interests of their pupils.

Part One: Teaching

A teacher must:

1. Set high expectations which inspire, motivate and challenge pupils

- establish a safe and stimulating environment for pupils, rooted in mutual respect
- set goals that stretch and challenge pupils of all backgrounds, abilities and dispositions
- demonstrate consistently the positive attitudes, values and behaviour which are expected of pupils.

2. Promote good progress and outcomes by pupils

- be accountable for pupils' attainment, progress and outcomes
- be aware of pupils' capabilities and their prior knowledge, and plan teaching to build on these
- guide pupils to reflect on the progress they have made and their emerging needs

- demonstrate knowledge and understanding of how pupils learn and how this impacts on teaching
- encourage pupils to take a responsible and conscientious attitude to their own work and study.

3. Demonstrate good subject and curriculum knowledge

- have a secure knowledge of the relevant subject(s) and curriculum areas, foster and maintain pupils' interest in the subject, and address misunderstandings
- demonstrate a critical understanding of developments in the subject and curriculum areas, and promote the value of scholarship
- demonstrate an understanding of and take responsibility for promoting high standards of literacy, articulacy and the correct use of standard English, whatever the teacher's specialist subject
- if teaching early reading, demonstrate a clear understanding of systematic synthetic phonics
- if teaching early mathematics, demonstrate a clear understanding of appropriate teaching strategies.

4. Plan and teach well structured lessons

- impart knowledge and develop understanding through effective use of lesson time
- promote a love of learning and children's intellectual curiosity
- set homework and plan other out-of-class activities to consolidate and extend the knowledge and understanding pupils have acquired
- reflect systematically on the effectiveness of lessons and approaches to teaching
- contribute to the design and provision of an engaging curriculum within the relevant subject area(s).

5. Adapt teaching to respond to the strengths and needs of all pupils

- know when and how to differentiate appropriately, using approaches which enable pupils to be taught effectively
- have a secure understanding of how a range of factors can inhibit pupils' ability to learn, and how best to overcome these

- demonstrate an awareness of the physical, social and intellectual development of children, and know how to adapt teaching to support pupils' education at different stages of development
- have a clear understanding of the needs of all pupils, including those with special educational needs; those of high ability; those with English as an additional language; those with disabilities; and be able to use and evaluate distinctive teaching approaches to engage and support them.

6. Make accurate and productive use of assessment

- know and understand how to assess the relevant subject and curriculum areas, including statutory assessment requirements
- make use of formative and summative assessment to secure pupils' progress
- use relevant data to monitor progress, set targets, and plan subsequent lessons
- give pupils regular feedback, both orally and through accurate marking, and encourage pupils to respond to the feedback.

7. Manage behaviour effectively to ensure a good and safe learning environment

- have clear rules and routines for behaviour in classrooms, and take responsibility for promoting good and courteous behaviour both in classrooms and around the school, in accordance with the school's behaviour policy
- have high expectations of behaviour, and establish a framework for discipline with a range of strategies, using praise, sanctions and rewards consistently and fairly
- manage classes effectively, using approaches which are appropriate to pupils' needs in order to involve and motivate them
- maintain good relationships with pupils, exercise appropriate authority, and act decisively when necessary.

8. Fulfil wider professional responsibilities

- make a positive contribution to the wider life and ethos of the school

- develop effective professional relationships with colleagues, knowing how and when to draw on advice and specialist support
- deploy support staff effectively
- take responsibility for improving teaching through appropriate professional development, responding to advice and feedback from colleagues
- communicate effectively with parents with regard to pupils' achievements and well-being.

Part Two: Personal and professional conduct

A teacher is expected to demonstrate consistently high standards of personal and professional conduct. The following statements define the behaviour and attitudes which set the required standard for conduct throughout a teacher's career.

- Teachers uphold public trust in the profession and maintain high standards of ethics and behaviour, within and outside school, by:
  - treating pupils with dignity, building relationships rooted in mutual respect, and at all times observing proper boundaries appropriate to a teacher's professional position
  - having regard for the need to safeguard pupils' well-being, in accordance with statutory provisions
  - showing tolerance of and respect for the rights of others
  - not undermining fundamental British values, including democracy, the rule of law, individual liberty and mutual respect, and tolerance of those with different faiths and beliefs
  - ensuring that personal beliefs are not expressed in ways which exploit pupils' vulnerability or might lead them to break the law.

Teachers must have proper and professional regard for the ethos, policies and practices of the school in which they teach, and maintain high standards in their own attendance and punctuality.

Teachers must have an understanding of, and always act within, the statutory frameworks which set out their professional duties and responsibilities.

ANSWERS

Pages 14–16

Stinky-pinkies

1. cocky jockey
2. numb chum
3. risky whisky
4. vicar's knickers
5. dahlia failure

Side-by-Side

1. pier; pierce
2. hors d'oeuvre; horse
3. captain; caption
4. stethoscope; Stetson
5. heroine; heron

Homophones

1. stationary; stationery
2. booze; boos
3. waist; waste
4. towed; toad
5. literal; littoral

Russian Dolls

1. peseta
2. garages
3. changeless
4. enamel
5. berate
6. scatty
7. macabre

Note: don't miss the excellent opportunities for spelling practice here.

Pages 44–45

1. 116 years
2. Ecuador
3. Sheep and horses
4. November
5. Squirrel fur
6. Dogs
7. Albert
8. Crimson
9. New Zealand
10. Orange

SOURCES

BOOKS

Anne Fine, *The Book of the Banshee* (Penguin, 1993)

Arthur Christopher Benson, *The Schoolmaster* (J. Murray, 1908)

David Hargreaves, *The Challenge for the Comprehensive School* (Routledge, 2014)

Doug Lemov, *Teach Like a Champion* (Jossey-Bass, c2010, and subsequent editions)

Frank McCourt, *Teacher Man* (Pearson Education, 2008)

Harper Lee, *To Kill a Mockingbird* (Penguin, 1985)

Howard Gardner, *Five Minds for the Future* (Harvard Business Press, 2008)

Ian McEwan, *The Children Act* (Doubleday, 2014)

Jan Mark, *Thunder and Lightnings* (Chivers Press, 1987, c1976)

Lucy Crehan, *Cleverlands* (Unbound, 2018)

Michael Rutter, *Fifteen Thousand Hours* (University of London Institute of Education, 1980)

Niall Ferguson, *Civilization* (Allen Lane, 2011)

Robert Bolt, *A Man for all Seasons* (Macmillan, 1985)

Tony Little, *An Intelligent Person's Guide to Education* (Bloomsbury Continuum, 2016)

T.S. Eliot, *Four Quartets* (Faber & Faber, 1960)

William Gibson, *Necromancer* (Gollancz, 1984)

William Wordsworth, *Intimations of Immortality from Recollections of Early Childhood* (Franklin Classics, 2018)

POETRY

Gervase Phinn, 'Less able', in *Classroom Creatures* (Roselea, 1996)

Miroslav Holub, 'A boy's head', in *Poems Before and After* (Bloodaxe Books, 2006)

The author and publishers have tried to trace the source of all materials used in the book. If any extract has not been properly acknowledged, then we shall be pleased to do so in a future edition.

ACKNOWLEDGEMENTS AND THANK YOU

To the following who have contributed variously to the text: Verity Lewin, Simon Knight, Emily Partridge, Neil Maslen, Simon Watson, Jane Branson, Peter Hyman, Marc Rowland, Juliette Jackson, Holly Manning, David Ingram, Cameron Mirza, Matt Young, Malcolm Wheeler, Samantha Smith; and especially Harry Hudson for his editing skills.

To the following for current examples of classroom practice: Garth Hill College, West London Free School, St Christopher's, Ecolint.

To the many thousands of teachers and children who have shared their classrooms, and the many hundreds of leaders who have welcomed me to their school communities.

To the friends and colleagues with whom I regularly exchange ideas on education.

OTHER TITLES BY ROY BLATCHFORD

Different Cultures (Longman, 2004)

Family Guide to Encouraging Young Readers (Scholastic, c1998)

Must Do Better (with Harry Hudson, John Catt Educational, 2022)

Practical Guide to the Headteachers' Standards (John Catt Educational, 2015)

Reflected Values (Simon & Schuster Education, 1995)

Self-Improving Schools (with Rebecca Clark, John Catt Educational, 2016)

Success Is a Journey (John Catt Educational, 2018)

The Forgotten Third (John Catt Educational, 2020)

The Primary Curriculum Leader's Handbook (John Catt Educational, 2019)

The Restless School (John Catt Educational, 2014)

The Secondary Curriculum Leader's Handbook (John Catt Educational, 2019)

The Teachers' Standards in the Classroom (Learning Matters, 2023 (5th edition))

The Three Minute Leader (John Catt Educational, 2020)

Values (Simon & Schuster Education, 1992)